Additional Praise
for *If You Say So*

"James Sweigert [is] not only a great man and mentor. He's a goddamn American hero."

— MITCH BOWERMAN,
Musical Artist, Mitch the Hero Inc.

If You Say So.

If You Say So.

MY STORY AND HOW I CHANGED IT TO SAVE MY LIFE.

JAMES SWEIGERT

Redwood Publishing, LLC

I dedicate this book to my mother, Mary.

This book is for the seekers.

Table of Contents

All Aboard!

M Y COUSIN DAVID DESMOND COACHED football for
a high school in Pasadena, California. It's a nice enough
spot—a neighborhood dotted with magnolia and eucalyptus
trees, the campus pushed up against the foothills, the sort of
place where kids train on bare trails and show up to class with
muddy sneakers—but for my cousin, and for this high school,
football is a big deal.

For David—for my whole family, really—football is our
sport. I grew up in Northern California, and we were 49ers
fans since before I can remember. My dad even took a job at
Kezar Stadium back when the team played there in the '40s.
I haven't always been happy with my dad's choices, but that's
one decision I can't fault him for. He and I loved the 49ers.
Football has that kind of effect on us. We bleed scarlet and gold.

So when David invited me to come watch one of his team's games, I happily braved the long commute from the Westside of Los Angeles. I didn't know any of the other coaches, the players, or the parents, and it was probably an hour or so outside of my neighborhood, even on a Saturday afternoon. But an invitation from a team's coach isn't something you take lightly. By all accounts, David's team had had a pretty lackluster year, and the players were about to face one of their league rivals—a team that had been playing very, very well and was clearly on its way to the playoffs.

When I got there that day, the feeling in the air was kind of resigned, as if everyone—the team, the cheer squad, even the fans—had read the papers and knew the visiting team was favored. Everyone seemed sure that the home team was about to take a loss.

My cousin steered me to the sidelines and stood me next to the team, probably because he knew I'd get a kick out of being close to the players. They looked pretty dispirited: they sat slumped on the bench, some with heads down. I took a look at the stands: not much of a spirited student presence either. The kids in attendance were obviously more interested in flirting with each other than in rooting for their team.

No one was psyched up. No one was even *trying* to psych themselves up. Everyone on the home team side seemed resigned to inevitable failure.

I looked across the field at the visiting team, only just stepping onto the field to begin warm-ups. The players' heads were held high and they were pumped up with the kind of confidence and enthusiasm that comes with a certainty that nothing can hurt you, that you can't possibly fail. They, too, had read the papers, and were sure that they were about to win—and win easily.

This was going to be a rout. Everyone believed it.

I stood on the sidelines next to the team as the game started. The visiting team ran a few plays, got a couple first downs, drove down the field, and scored, as expected. The home team received the kickoff, ran a few plays, quickly went four and out, and had to punt the ball back to the rivals. The visiting team, still pumped, still excited, eager, and ready to win, ran another series of plays . . . and then something unexpected happened. A couple of kids on the home team made one or two really good tackles, stopping the visitors from getting to their next first down.

I started to get excited.

I stepped up to the sideline and started yelling for these kids, my voice cracking with enthusiasm: "YOU CAN STOP THESE GUYS!" I shouted. "COME ON! YOU JUST DID IT! YOU JUST STOPPED THEM!" I'm naturally an energetic, enthusiastic person, and this sort of thing qualified as a damn-good moment in my book, so I was getting into it, jumping around, clapping and shouting at the field, "LOOK WHAT YOU JUST DID! YOU CAN STOP THESE GUYS!"

The players on the bench started looking over at me. I wasn't a teacher. I wasn't a parent. Who was this crazy guy shouting at the team? Nobody knew who I was, but I was yelling for them. I was cheering them on, way more than any of their teammates, family, or friends. Just an enthusiastic sports fan.

You know the thing about enthusiasm? It's infectious. The more I shouted, the louder I got, the more those players started to listen and believe that they actually *could* stop the visiting team's offense. "My God, he's right," they started saying to each other. "We just stopped them."

The body language of the defensive squad started to shift. The players grew more alert, their shoulders rolled back. There was a new determination and strength in the way they looked on the field: they had started to believe in themselves. My enthusiasm was spreading to the whole team. A few of the coaches saw what I was doing and they, too, started to join in, almost as if I was reminding them to be optimistic.

The offensive squad members took their cue from their teammates and started thinking that maybe they had a real chance; maybe it was time to actually go for it. After all, the defense was stepping up. They got hold of the ball and got in a four-yard run, and that set me off all over again: "YOU CAN MOVE THE BALL ON THESE GUYS! YOU JUST

PROVED IT TO YOURSELVES! YOU CAN MOVE THE
BALL ON THESE GUYS! LET'S GO!"

The kids on the home team weren't the only ones to notice,
of course. The visiting team quickly saw that, yep, the ball
was moving in the wrong direction, and yep, their opponents
were somehow a lot more determined and resolute than they'd
expected. I was just pointing out something that anyone could
have noticed—that the home team really did have the talent
and the grit to get this done—but now that I'd called attention
to it, it was the only thing the visitors could see. I yelled again,
"YOU'VE GOT THEM ON THEIR HEELS!" They started to
falter—*Oh my god, he's right; they're moving the ball on us*—and
in a few quick moments, the home team had driven through
and scored a touchdown. My words were getting in their heads.

The energy changed in the stands. The crowd almost
seemed surprised. All of a sudden, people started paying attention. They were standing up and shouting right along with
me, "YOU'VE GOT THIS! LET'S GO!!"

Eventually, the athletic director for the home team came
down to the field and asked me who I was. I told her I was
David Desmond's cousin and that I loved football. She nodded,
and I soon had her next to me, her hands on her knees, yelling
with me and clapping at every play.

That day, I shouted until I lost my voice, but the home team
took the game. No one is saying that positive reinforcement is

the *only* thing you need in life—but the complete shift in the team's attitude, self-perception, and energy came from, I'm not embarrassed to say, one crazy guy on the sidelines shouting encouragement at them, believing in them. They snatched a victory from what started out as a pretty certain loss, and a major part of that victory came from the way they thought about themselves and the language they were using to think about themselves. They believed the hype—both negative, and then, positive.

My experience with the home team that day revealed to me the power of the spoken word. I saw how easily it could affect other people's lives, and I realized that the philosophy I'd already applied to my own life could help others: if it can work on a team of high school football players, already focused on a game they're sure they'll lose, it can work on anybody.

The story you tell yourself about your life is a self-fulfilling prophecy.

Or, as I like to tell people, you will be happy and successful, or you will not. *If you say so.*

* * *

It can be tempting to think that we're always at the mercy of our circumstances. My own background isn't an especially happy one—I had a pretty rough home life during childhood, and an early adulthood scarred by depression, alcoholism, and addiction—but the truth is that the way you think and talk about yourself, the way you frame your personal story, has more of an effect on your circumstances than you probably think.

For years, I didn't know how to think about my family. My relationships with my father, my stepfather, and even my mother were all pretty difficult, and I know now that the love and validation I kept turning to them for was hard for them to give. Don't get the wrong idea—none of these people were villains—but I'm the youngest of seven siblings.

Then, when I was seven, my new stepfather moved in, bringing with him five more stepsiblings. My mother also ran a daycare facility out of the house. It was complete pandemonium. I don't think any of my family really had the time to process this "merger," or had the motivation to invest in me or my future. We were all in survival mode. Life wears people out; I know that now. But as a kid, I had emotional needs that were never met, and that's the sort of thing that deposits a fair-sized chip on a person's shoulder.

I spent years ruminating on the abuse, the sadness, and the crippling addiction, trapped by blinders of my own making. It took a radical shift in perspective for me to step off that path and start working toward a new life. And working toward a new life requires tremendous vision, no matter what result you're looking for. I'd spent years working in film and television production, but what I really wanted was a chance to stretch creatively and work on the bigger, more important projects, tell the stories that I knew had value. To do that, I needed a job as an executive producer. I wanted to run my own production company.

They don't hand out EP credits like candy. It's a relatively exclusive club. But I believe in vision boards. I believe in the power of affirmative thinking. I had heard the production company I wanted to work for was hiring. I had worked my way up from the bottom and had been producing for a few years, and I wanted to make the leap to the next level. I went to meet the owners of the company, and, as I was leaving, I snatched one of their business cards. I brought the card home, scanned it, and turned it into a Photoshop file. Then, I redesigned the card by adding my name with the title below: *executive producer*. I posted that card on the door to my bedroom, so that I would see it every time I walked in. That was my first real step on the path to success.

Three and a half months later, I came out of a meeting with the owners of the company, ready to print up copies of my fantasy business card—but now, for real. The executive producer job was mine. I'd told myself that it was within reach, that I had what it took to get there, and now I'd done it. A significant part of that achievement we can chalk up to my own natural chutzpah and hard work, but a not-inconsiderable part of it can be traced back to the Law of Attraction, as described in the works of Esther and Jerry Hicks, also known as Abraham-Hicks.

Visualization, meditation, gratitude, vision boards, self-affirmations, personal mantras: all play a serious role in propelling us out of our past and into our dreams. Once I'd won that job, I started to make more money than I'd ever imagined. I literally doubled my income two years in a row just by believing that money comes to me frequently and easily. I bought my dream home near the beach in Marina del Rey. Later, when I realized I wanted a yard for my amazing dog, Duke Kahanamoku, I put a new dream home on my vision board. I added a few images of a beautiful, new, gated home up in the hills with a black gate. I constantly looked at those images and visualized living in that beautiful gated home in the hills above Hollywood, and now I live in that new home in Beverly Hills. Far from the tumultuous relationships of my childhood, I'm now partnered with an incredible woman who matches me in temperament, drive, and affection. I live cleanly, and I do what I say I'm going to do when I say I'm going to do it. And it's easy. It's easy because I say it's easy. I have come to learn that when I live in this way, and practice these actions, that everything I want is downstream. That is the power of the spoken word. If you say so.

But here's the thing: It's not just positive thinking. It's not just mantras and vision boards. These things are important tools, but if you can't back them up with real effort and willingness to change and grow, they won't get you anywhere.

I mentor a lot of people, and I tell them that life is like a train—one of those coal-powered beasts, a steam engine roaring through time, building speed with each shovelful of coal, chugging past verdant valleys and peaceful vistas, climbing mountains and sometimes wheezing to the peaks, only to rocket down again. You've got the Steam Locomotive with the furnace; the fire is the passion inside you, your soul's desire. The Coal Car, which contains the fuel, is the work that you must do yourself. The Passenger Car is the way you think about the people in your life. The Baggage Car is filled with personal history that you can always unload at the next train station. From the Observation Car, you can safely take in and understand the world around you through meditation and philosophy. In the Dining Car, you learn to care for yourself. In the Bar Car, you learn to accept your addictions. And the Caboose is the vantage point from which you can reflect on your life and appreciate your achievements.

You've got to stay on your own tracks, as trying to get on someone else's tracks will just derail the both of you and lead to a train wreck. I have been there. Every so often you'll pull into a station, where you can have a moment of peace and safety to unload baggage, but for the most part, you have everything you need on that train. Traveling safely is about making sure that you are shoveling the coal and that you stay on the rails God has laid out for you.

The first time I got derailed was in high school. Early on, I spent a little too much time in the Bar Car. My friends and I would sneak beer from one of the neighbor's refrigerators and walk down to the railroad tracks near the state college. There, we'd drink Mickey's big mouths and watch the trains go by. We would sit in the shade of the eucalyptus trees and feel the earth shake as these powerful, monstrous locomotives and their loads rumbled past. I'd spend the whole day drinking malt liquor and getting hammered. For me, it was escape. It was freedom.

And it sounds beautiful—a kid setting out with a six pack of Mickey's, leaving behind a difficult home life and truly embracing everything the world had to offer, coming back refreshed and beer-happy. It was everything I told myself I needed.

It happened, however, that most of the stories I told myself were wrong. My stories were all lies. But let's not get ahead of ourselves.

CHAPTER 1

The Steam Engine Locomotive

I GREW UP IN SACRAMENTO, CALIFORNIA, which was where, in 1869, the "Big Four"— Hopkins, Stanford, Crocker, and Huntington—formed the Central Pacific Railroad Company. With the hard labor of Chinese immigrants, they laid 690 miles of track to Promontory Point, Utah, to create the first transcontinental railroad.

That history was embedded in the landscape. In fact, I grew up on Huntington Road, named for Collis Potter Huntington, who had made his name selling supplies and hardware for miners in the city before forming the Big Four. Sacramento was a hub for many of the train lines that moved produce and people around the West, and we had a large train yard and a beautiful train station downtown, just northeast of where the Big Four had their shops.

When I was a kid, I loved seeing the trains pull into the station. They were mammoth feats of engineering, all power and purpose. A train would pull into the station, braking and creating the kind of noise that only those giant steel beasts can make, and people would flock to it. On cold days, you could see the steam rising off of it—a huge, monstrous machine, big enough to consume you without thought, but harnessed to the conductor's will. Watching the trains made me feel powerful, as if the fact that a person could control this terrible beast meant that maybe I could control the chaos in my own life.

And that's really the attraction of a train—all that mighty power. All that determination. The tracks are already laid, the destination is predetermined, and the only thing that can get you from Here to There is an engine. An engine whose only purpose is to move *forward*. Whose only mandate is *move*. Knowing how your engine works—what fuels it, and how you keep it fighting fit—is your job as the conductor. It's a crucial job too. Any little mistake can lead to derailment and potential disaster.

I've been around long enough to know that getting derailed is almost inevitable. Sure, there probably do exist people who power through life with a cowcatcher out in front, knocking obstacles and debris out of their way, people whose tracks have been laid so neatly and so simply that deviating from them is unthinkable. I'm not one of those people. It took me a long time to figure out how to make my engine run.

I was always a creative kid. My mom was busy and over-whelmed, and she never seemed to have enough time or energy for me. I'm the youngest of seven kids, and after my parents divorced, my mom remarried, this time to a man who had his own brood of five children, so our household went from seven kids to twelve in the time it took two people to say "I do." My blood siblings were all older, so I think they coped better with her sudden distraction, but it was never easy for me.

And I felt the loss of my father keenly. Soon after I was born, I was told that my dad had left us for another woman. I was seven years old when a new man came to take his place, bringing five kids with him. To distract me and keep me out of her hair, my mom would always make sure to supply me with No. 2 pencils and binder paper to doodle on. I will always be grateful to her for that. I learned to draw pretty early on, as it was one of the few escapes for me—a quiet, self-contained activity that I could do without having to engage anyone, especially my new stepsiblings.

But drawing wasn't what was expected of me. My maternal grandfather was a state senator, and my dad's father was a federal judge in San Francisco, appointed to the bench by Eisenhower himself. Five of my uncles were successful attorneys in Sacramento. In a lot of ways, we were kind of the Kennedys of Sacramento—conservative-leaning Democrats, Irish Catholic, endlessly politically involved, and deeply dysfunctional. My artistic tendencies set me apart from the rest of my family, and none of them knew how to approach a kid who preferred doodling to morning walk-and-talks. And it wasn't any better outside my family. I attended parochial schools that offered no art classes at the time; they were focused on academics, and while I get the societal value of that kind of curriculum, it was in no way set up to respond to my needs.

No one really knew what to do with me. I had brothers who were all college graduates, on track to becoming successful doctors, lawyers, and businessmen—brothers who seemed fated to fit in with the expectations of my power-brokering family. They had listened whenever my grandmother, Edna Desmond, told us, "Remember who you are and what you represent." But it was clear from an early age that that path was not for me. I was always the youngest, always the awkward, artsy one, always the kid you could overlook or forget about. And because I didn't have anyone who looked out for me, who could have guided me toward a sense of purpose that fit my skills and temperament, I constantly felt like *I* was the problem. The stories I told myself, stories I created after various "events" in my childhood—that I was unlovable, that I didn't deserve kindness or affection because I just couldn't get my act together long enough to earn those things, as my brothers had—those stories shaped my outlook on life for a very long time. Eventually, I just accepted the "fact" that happiness was something I'd have to learn to live without, because it sure as shit wasn't something the world felt obliged to give me.

By the time I got to high school, I was deeply troubled and depressed, and I started drinking alcohol regularly. I loved beer and rum; Bacardi and Coke was a favorite. Then, prodded by some cool dudes who were staying with us, I started smoking pot. By sophomore year I was snorting cocaine, and by junior year I was dealing it at the very prestigious all-boys Catholic high school I attended, the same esteemed institution that all of my older brothers had graduated from many years before. Senior year, I really hit bottom. I was diagnosed with chronic ulcerative colitis and nearly died, so I spent a long time with death on my mind. I thought I would never live up to my family's expectations, so I wrote a suicide note, just to see if it would knock anything loose. I knew by then that I didn't fit in and never would—not with my school and not with my family, whom it seemed I never stopped disappointing. Alcohol, and eventually a cornucopia of pharmacological experiments, were my only comforts, my only reprieve from this near-constant parade of reasons to loathe myself.

I do think that if it weren't for my use of drugs and alcohol during that time, I would have made good on that suicide note. They kept me numb and thus alive at a time when staying alive was far from my highest priority. I knew that I couldn't trust people; my relationships with my siblings, both step- and blood-related, were far from bastions of safety. I was the youngest and the smallest of twelve kids, remember, and they all made sure I knew how much bigger and more powerful than me they were. So I put mental walls up. I developed a venomous tongue, and I made sure that I was always on guard, that no one would get the better of me.

Another event that carried me through those difficult years was the chance meeting of a boy named Ross Perich during my freshman year. Ross and I became fast friends, and he brought me home one day to meet his mother, Noradele. They took me in, and I spent a lot of my high school years there to escape the tumult of my own home. Noradele became a second mother to me and, to this day, I still call her "Mom."

But Ross and Noradele couldn't help me escape completely. When I was nineteen, still bunking with my mom and stepfather, they came home early one night and caught me in bed with my girlfriend, Vikki Madsen. She was my first love. There wasn't a lot I could say. The Catholic Church has a pretty clear stance on premarital sex, and my mom and stepfather were horrified. Vikki was mortified, embarrassed, and ashamed. As I recall, they threw us both out on the spot, sending us out into the cold night through a side door. I barely had time to get my jeans on.

That incident marked the beginning of a period in my life when I slept in a park under a grove of redwood trees in a green nylon sleeping bag. Then, after a cop suggested politely that I move along, I found a sheltered bench in McKinley Park. I had bottles of booze hidden around downtown Sacramento, and I would skateboard to each one and take hits off of them to get through the lonely days and to kill the pain. At one point, I squatted in an apartment with a bunch of other people, a place downtown, on H Street. But when the rains came, the roof caved in, and I was back out on the streets.

I'd had an alcohol habit since adolescence, but as my life got harder, I began drinking more, smoking pot daily, and doing more cocaine. I even sold coke for a while, running around town with a 9-millimeter handgun in a shoulder holster, thinking I was Tony Montana. I was out of my mind. I did unspeakable things to people, things I'm ashamed of—some that I don't even remember, but that I'd be reminded about the next day by fellow acquaintances. But I quit that life when the DEA popped half the crew we were associated with. Some went to prison; some were killed on the streets. I believe the only reason I avoided jail time was that the cops were working off tapped phone calls, and when the transcripts were read, I was grateful I never used my real name. I was chased by the cops on multiple occasions, but I rode a fast motorcycle that I could easily sneak onto the American River Parkway, and disappear. I was reckless but I never got caught. I used to say, "You don't have to be faster than the bear, you just have to be faster than the guy you're with."

But I just couldn't seem to stop drinking. I had become a completely self-centered alcoholic. Life was *so* rotten and *so* miserable. And I believed—in fact, I was sure—that every horror, every moment of misery and despair, was exactly what I deserved. I'd made a disastrously wrong decision years ago, back when I was seven and my mom was trying to cope with five new stepkids who all needed her attention. I looked back, and it was at that point in my life when something snapped and that's when I *really* got angry.

If I'd only been a good little boy, my reasoning went, if I'd been right, or better somehow, I'd have figured out that I was destined to become a doctor or a lawyer or a real estate broker, someone my mom could be proud of. I'd be in college, with a scholarship, and I'd have the kind of future that makes grown men slap you on the back and recommend investment opportunities. I wouldn't be dicking around with my art and creativity. I'd be a good person. And my parents would love me. The fact that I was unhappy, that I couldn't rely on any of my family members, obviously meant that I had chosen poorly. The problem was me. I deserved this homelessness and addiction and crippling depression. I deserved it because I was a bad kid.

The worst part was that I couldn't seem to stop drinking, no matter how hard I tried. I'd have a moment when I knew that something was wrong, and I'd throw the bottle away, certain that that would fix it, that I'd just clean myself up and go get help. But half an hour later I'd be back in the liquor store, picking out another bottle.

And then, one night, I decided I meant it. I was done with booze, for real this time. No more. *Finito.* End of story. I can't remember the exact circumstances, but I know that that night, it was cold and I eventually justified having *just one.* It was on. I drank until I was blackout drunk. At about 2:30 a.m., still in a blackout, I was speeding somewhere downtown and I went off the road and wrapped my truck around a tree or a telephone pole. To this day, I still don't know what I hit. I came to and stumbled out of the cab to look at the damage. The fender was warped beyond all recognition, and the engine was bent but somehow was still running, making a horrible noise. One of my headlights was pointing to the sky, but that engine was still going. I should have been dead.

I threw the bent fender and my license plate in the back of the truck, put it in gear, pulled back onto the road, and then blacked out again. I know now that I was leaving the scene of a drunk-driving accident, which is illegal in and of itself, let alone driving under the influence. At the time, I was too drunk to think or care about the police. All I could think about was that I'd come *this* close to death, and that maybe it was a mistake. Maybe I was supposed to die that night.

I headed home—a tiny place downtown whose deposit I'd paid with cocaine cash—and parked in the middle of the street. Still drunk, I decided to kill myself. I was twenty-five years old and I had decided to die. I had a Remington 870 pump-action shotgun, but I was out of shells, so that was out.

I'd have to find some other way to get it done. Wrist slitting? Seemed really messy. Hanging? I didn't have my lariat in the apartment.

Eventually, I settled on electrocution. I decided to fill the tub, get in, and then drag the television set into the water with me. I had seen it work on TV. I have the clearest recollection of standing over the bathtub, weeping, still profoundly drunk, watching the water pour from the faucet, and marveling at how it was somehow not filling the tub. I'd forgotten to stop up the drain, of course, but I was in no frame of mind to understand what was happening. The only thing I took away from watching the water swirl down the drain was, "I can't even fucking kill myself." I'd somehow managed to fuck up the one thing that I could do to make the world a better place.

I don't remember making the call to my sister Patricia, but she saved my life. She called my brother David, who showed up somewhere around 3:00 a.m. I heard a knock at the door and I came to. The experience of the suicide attempt was enough to somewhat sober me up. I will never forget his eyes when I answered the door. They were wider than I'd ever seen them. After I'd rambled to my sister something about suicide, he was terrified he would show up and find his little brother dead.

He came inside and gave me one of the kindest, most important gifts I've ever received: he listened when I needed him most. He listened to me whine and blame my dad for leaving. He listened to me complain about our mom and stepdad subjecting us to endless chaos. He listened to me blame our stepsiblings for being "jerks." He listened to me complain about the rest of our family—even him—for growing up, moving out, and leaving me behind. He even listened as I finally blamed God for every problem I could think of.

And then, as my drunken blame-game rant came to a close, on an inhale, I gasped, "I need help."

He put me to bed and tucked me in. The next morning, he woke me, and he and I sat down together, and we opened up the Yellow Pages to "A" for "Alcohol." For years I had known I was an alcoholic, but had never been ready to admit it.

"It's a progressive disease," he told me, looking at the ad for the National Council on Alcoholism and Drug Dependence. "If you're already trying to kill yourself, what else do you have to lose?"

I couldn't argue with him. It had become clear that for me, to drink was to die.

The National Council on Alcoholism and Drug Dependence tried to set me up with a treatment center, but I didn't have any money or health insurance, so they recommended a twelve-step program.

"It's free," they said, "and it helps a lot of people."

Free fit my budget, but I didn't know what to expect. I don't think anyone does, at first. And I was so scared, I begged David to go to the first meeting with me. And he did. I had no place else to go. I was a terrified little boy inside a twenty-five-year-old man's body. He came with me, and we sat in the back row, and no matter how scared I was—that I'd be called up to speak or judged, or maybe forced into electroshock therapy—I could look over and know that he was there for me. My brother was there. He was my Eskimo.*

So much of the story I've told myself has been about being alone and feeling isolated, even within a giant family. I've spent years ruminating on how that solitude quashed my belief in myself, crushed my sense of self-worth, and annihilated any ideas I had that my artistic talents were of any value. The truth is that those years of isolation were real. The time I spent feeling overwhelmed and unloved and forgotten—that wasn't a figment of my imagination. It really happened. But it's also true that in this situation, my brother was there for me. He let me lean on him in a way no one had ever done before, and I will always be grateful to him for it.

Getting into a program designed to help me stay away from alcohol (and avoid death, as I'd discovered) ended up

---

* The term Eskimo comes from a parable about a man who was out in the tundra hunting in the winter. He gets stuck and thinks he's going to freeze to death there all alone. Out of nowhere, an Eskimo appears and saves him. It became a term now used in the twelve-step program, and refers to the people who save us.

being one of the foundational pieces of the life I lead today. I learned to be honest with my peers and with myself, to be open-minded and to look for ways in which I could be willing to change. I met several wise people who'd survived long enough to know what I was up against, who could advise me on getting healthy, and on finding the people who could support me in my journey. I had to clean up my messes and get flat with the universe. I had to ask for forgiveness and do some forgiving of my own. I have grown immeasurably under their watchful eyes, so much so that for many years, I've been mentoring people myself. It is the greatest gift to watch lives transform before your very eyes. I have seen miracles in the work I do. I have seen men become better husbands, better fathers and sons, better brothers, better boyfriends, and better employers. I've watched them become men with integrity. *Real* men.

One of the most important things these wise men taught me was that I could do whatever I wanted to do. That the careers my family advocated for—the respectable vocations that would make the grandfathers proud—weren't everything. It wasn't the only perspective in the world. I could think about my creativity from an entirely different perspective, one that valued visual expression, one that understood the skills I'd been developing. The fact that I wasn't a lawyer or a doctor wasn't a blight on my reputation or a failure of the family. I could pursue my passions, I could follow my talent, and it didn't have to have anything to do with my family's judgment. They could approve or disapprove, and it didn't need to affect me. My friend Jimi says, "I'm not for everyone." I aspire to not give a fuck as well as he does.

I'd always been drawn to entertainment, and I'd always been quick with a joke, as a kid, I'd relied on my wit to make people laugh and get me out of altercations with my nine older brothers. I used to love watching comics on TV, like Jonathan Winters and impersonator Rich Little. I loved *The Flip Wilson Show* and the characters he would portray, such as Geraldine. I would make people laugh by impersonating his characters. Later, I would crack up my friends by impersonating Richard Pryor and George Carlin and doing their bits. Anything for attention. Comedy was a natural fit, as were screenwriting and filmmaking. So, armed with newfound confidence that I didn't need to be ashamed of my artistic leanings, I wrote, produced, and directed a short film. It even got into some film festivals.

I had found the spark. The spark that turns to flame when nourished and encouraged. That roaring fire in the furnace that powers me. I had finally figured out the way to get my engine to rumble in life and to start moving forward. That engine—my creativity—had always been with me, ever since my mom tried to placate me with No. 2 pencils and binder paper, ever since I'd been able to lose myself in my drawings to nurture an imagination that came to life on the page.

Before getting sober, I'd convinced myself that the best way to make the world a better place was to erase myself from it. But the reality was that by making art, by drawing, designing, painting, writing, and filming, I was embroidering the world, helping to make it a more beautiful place.

The beautiful part of knowing that my engine is built from art is knowing that just by being true to myself and following my passions, I'm traveling in the right direction. I'm constantly fulfilled when I am doing what I love. I recently traveled to Portugal, where I was exposed to amazing architecture that was inspired by architectural traditions and innovations from countries and cultures all around the world. Here was a building that was erected to showcase English and French styles of architecture, and here was one that was inspired by Roman and Spanish styles. Here was one that clearly displays a Moorish influence. Portugal is full of castles and buildings and cathedrals designed by people who had seen what other architects in Europe, Asia, and Africa were doing and were inspired to go even further. It is art built on art built on art.

I hadn't built a sandcastle since I was a little boy on vacation on the beaches of Santa Cruz, but when I came home from my trip to Portugal, I grabbed a shovel and a bucket, and trooped on down to the tide line. When I got there, I started building. I tried to mimic the architectural styles I'd seen on my trip. I wasn't great at it at first, but I kept at it, and I got pretty good. Since then I have built some magnificent sandcastles.

Nowadays, I keep my hand in, but I mostly like to build them for friends or weddings on the beach. There's no permanence to a sandcastle, so it's not like I can sell them or turn them into a business. I build them for fun, but I also build them because my soul's desire is to create. That primal urge to create art, even if that creation will be washed away by the evening tide, drives me forward.

As an artist, I'm always keen to inspire creativity in other people. Even if your story is that you aren't artistic, I believe that you have the same creative spark that I've found at my own core. It may not be the thing that drives you—it may not be the fire in your engine—but I'd be remiss if I didn't at least encourage you to start out by grabbing some clay and exploring with your hands. Create! You don't have to be great to start, but you can start to be great.

Creativity comes in many forms. Personally, I believe that creating something is a form of meditation, and an effort to uncover the parts of ourselves that we've kept buried. If you don't know how your engine works—if you don't know what truly drives you—taking the time to work with your hands, to build something beautiful or useful, can reveal some aspect of your engine. I'm not saying it'll happen all at once. It took years for me to uncover the value of my own drive. But it might give you a glimpse of what lies ahead.

I spent *so much* of my youth convinced of a story that wasn't true. I let the world tell me who I was, depending on the observations and biases of others for my own self-esteem. I let this go on so long that I lost sight of the part of my life that gives me purpose. Someone once passed an axiom along to me: "The longest journey a man can make is from his head to his heart." If my life isn't an illustration of that truth, I don't know what is. The stories we tell ourselves about who we are and the way life has treated us will always affect the way we behave. If we say so. If you tell yourself that all risks are dangerous and never pan out, you will never take risks, whereas if you tell yourself that some results are worth a little uncertainty, and that you've always got a chance of coming out on top, you'll be more likely to take a chance on something risky. Being open to the possibility of a windfall means that you are, inevitably, more likely to receive one. When you think about all of the things you ever worried about that never happened, then there should be just as much of a chance that it will all work out swimmingly, right? You lose all the games you don't play, after all. You have to remember that you were intended to flourish, to find happiness and fulfill your incredible potential, even when your brain tries to tell you otherwise. Life can be amazing. If you say so.

By the same token, I spent years looping the story in my head that I was unlovable, sure that I was miserable because I was a disappointment to my parents and family. I had chosen to be the wrong sort of person. It was only after I learned that I had a story and that I could change that story—that I could come to see myself as a valuable member of society, someone with many things to live for—that I was able to address my problems. I have been clean and sober for more than thirty years now, and I've been able to stick to my sobriety not because it was easy to maintain—addictions never make anything easy—but because I changed the way I speak about my relationship with alcohol and drugs. Because I changed the way I speak about my life and I focus on what is good and what is working for me today.

I've worked hard to pay forward what my mentors have done for me. What they continue to do for me. Over the past thirty years, I've gotten calls to help so many celebrities, rock stars, Hollywood executives, and other successful people stay off of TMZ, out of jail, and out of their own heads—to clean up their lives and change their stories for the better. Everyone should have the opportunity to tap into their true potential and build an amazing life, whether that means making a big name for themselves or being an amazing second-grade teacher in Akron, Ohio. That's why I'm writing this book: to help you make that long, fraught journey from your head to your heart, and find the place where the universe intended you to be. I believe God wants you to flourish and be amazing! I'm here to help as many people as I can to feel fulfilled, with a sense of purpose and personal achievement, to be able to build wealth and connect with other human beings, to feel loved and find happiness. That's what I've set out to do in these pages and beyond.

Change is possible. You can crack yourself open to a life you've never dreamed of—and it doesn't have to be hard. But you have to change your story before you can change your life.

CHAPTER 2

The Coal Car

DARKNESS, AND THE SENSATION OF movement. Behind you, flashes of light from the outside world flicker as your train rumbles past fields and forests, concrete cityscapes, and the blinking brightness of sunlight over open water. But none of that makes its way into the Coal Car. Here, the only light comes from the glowing embers of the furnace in the locomotive. Red and gaping, the furnace is ever-hungry, and the heat it emits withers your hair and draws beads of sweat from your skin. You are soot-covered, sweating, and in constant danger of losing your footing. Should the train take a curve too quickly, you could tumble into the mound of coal on either side of the furnace, or, God forbid, against the blistering furnace itself. But this is no time to let your fears overwhelm you. You have a job to do.

You hoist your shovel from the mound, a healthy pile of coal cradled in its basket, and you fling the payload into the furnace with a clang. The furnace must be fed. Keeping that fire burning is the only thing—*the only thing*—that powers the train. If you were to stop, or even just pause, the train would puff to a halt, stalled in the snow, all forward momentum lost.

In the last chapter, we talked about finding whatever it is that makes up your engine. In this chapter, we'll talk about the less glamorous part of forward motion: the work you must do to power that engine. Where the engine is everything we want to be, everything we yearn for, the Coal Car is the fuel, all the necessary day-to-day business of staying alive and maintaining the energy we need to keep going.

For most of us, that coal translates to our job. It means bringing in enough money to pay the rent, pay the gas bill, buy the groceries, add to our savings. It is the everyday maintenance that none of us can neglect. I mentor a young man who's going after his master's degree and trying to balance it with a part-time job; he's got classes to attend and hours to work and homework to get through—and though none of it is his engine, it's all important. If he lets any part of it slip, everything falls apart. When he calls to check in, knowing he's busy, I ask how it's going. He replies, "Shoveling coal, boss, shoveling coal!" It's our shorthand, but I know he's doing the work he needs to do to take care of himself.

But it's more than a fear of letting something slide; it's about knowing that humanity is at its best when we're working. When we're contributing. We are at our best when we're striving for something, whether it's creating a podcast, building a house, or filming a movie. Productivity makes us feel whole.

Every so often I come across guys who are new to sobriety, and they haven't yet figured out how to shovel coal. They hang out at the back of the room, watching the bustle of relationships around them, and they've got nothing to grab onto. I try to cut them a break.

I reach out, shake their hand, and ask, "So what's your story?"

They aren't sure how to answer that. They don't even know they have one.

"What are you up to?" I ask.

"Nothing," they say. And what they mean is, *No one told me I had to be doing something.*

"You working?" I go on, trying to drop a hint.

"No, I'm just—"

Yeah, I know how that goes.

When I finally got sober, I quickly found that if I wasn't doing something, I'd end up thinking about drinking or doing drugs, and that was a great way to get into mischief and make myself miserable. This is why shoveling coal isn't about the results. It's not about the rent or the gas bill being paid, or having groceries in the fridge. It's about doing those things *yourself.* For yourself.

If someone came along and just gave you enough money to pay for everything you need, you'd still be miserable. Not because there's anything especially toxic about having your needs met, because there isn't; the old story that you have to know poverty to understand your blessings is just a lie people made up to let themselves off the hook for watching homeless people die in the street. We distinguish between needs and wants for a reason, and you don't get extra credit for struggling to pay your bills. No, the toxic part of having someone wave a magic wand and make everything easy is that *your work is inherently valuable.* Not just to your employer, but also to you. And a magic wand steals that value. I heard someone once say, "If you want to know what God thinks of money, just look at some of the people he gives it to."

The sweat and the sore muscles and the knowledge that you spent the day productively all do more for you than just ensure a paycheck. They give you satisfaction in yourself. They raise your chin a quarter inch, give you self-esteem. They give you a good night's sleep. They occupy your mind and keep you from whatever self-destructive behaviors you might tend toward. Work keeps you functioning. It allows you to put your head on the pillow at night and fall asleep knowing you are participating in life. It keeps you sane.

It took me a long time to figure out my engine. Figuring out my Coal Car wasn't much easier. You can imagine that before I went into recovery, my ability to hold down any kind of steady job was pretty limited. I had temporary enterprises (for example, my failed stint in recreational pharmaceutical sales), but nothing reliable. Nothing that could get me up in the morning, sure that my efforts were going to have tangible results. Nothing that I knew was going to give me enough of an income to let me plan for the future or take care of a partner (though, to be fair, the future was the furthest thing from my mind, and anyone I partnered with was in much the same situation as I was).

But because I was doing nothing to build my place in the world, because I wasn't moving forward in my life, I knew that the world could be cavalier about sloughing me off. Who would miss me if I were gone? I didn't have a boss to inconvenience. I didn't have a girlfriend to cry over my grave. I wasn't on speaking terms with either of my parents—and as one of a dozen siblings, I couldn't imagine that they would have cared anyway. I was perpetually on the downswing. Disposable.

Getting into recovery pushed me to go looking for my self-worth. The men who mentored me encouraged me to chase after career choices I'd never given myself permission to pursue before, and that was when my life began to change. One of my first teachers was a gentle man named Eric Balme, a marriage and family therapist. He was the first one to really sit down with me and help me unpack my life and start to take a look at it. When I told him about my family, Eric gave me some advice that I still find myself returning to: "Go where you get fed," he told me during one of our midafternoon café meetings. "You don't go into a Chinese restaurant and order tacos. They don't serve them there. You're seeking love and validation from people who aren't giving it to you. So find a better place. Figure out where you get that good feeling, the feeling of being around people who make you a better you, and go there. Put your energies *there*." He wasn't wrong. My family didn't seem to give *themselves* much validation or approval, so there wasn't a chance in hell that they'd ever give it to me.

A big part of shoveling coal—of going about the daily business of living your life—is knowing what boosts you and keeps you moving, and knowing how to avoid situations that drag you down. It's not just earning a paycheck. It's doing whatever you need to do to sustain yourself and push yourself to grow.

In my early twenties, I had once done stand-up comedy—drunk, as a dare—and it was freeing and exhilarating and terrifying all at once. But I'd never thought that it could be something I'd do on a more permanent basis. It wasn't one of the grandma-approved careers.

But the people I met in recovery told me that I could do whatever I want to do. They told me that my alcoholism and my depression weren't death sentences. They said I had survived the hardest part, and now it was time to live! I had thought of myself as "broken," but that meant precisely squat for a person who was just figuring out that the story he'd been telling himself was nothing more than a vicious lie. My being "broken" was part of that lie, and I was free to toss all that bullshit aside. Kick it to the curb. I was free to start creating a new story about myself. One full of truth and love.

So I said, "To hell with it," and I signed up for an open-mic night at the Metro Bar & Grill, an underground club in downtown Sacramento. And I started telling stories, doing impersonations, and telling jokes. A lot of them were awful—everyone who does stand-up starts out badly; there's no way to avoid it—but it wasn't like I had anything riding on my success other than finding a new way to grow. I was twenty-five years old, and the old-timers were telling me, "Just go for it. Do whatever you want to do." I'd always loved movies and storytelling, and everything started to coalesce as I realized I could keep doing everything I loved, and that I didn't need to hold myself to the impossible standard my family had seemingly always held me to. One evening, I went to the theater to see a new foreign film, *Cinema Paradiso*. It lit me up. *This is beautiful visual storytelling*, I realized. *And it's limitless.* I knew then I wanted to do that.

Star Wars had a profound impact on me as a kid, when I saw it during its original theatrical release. It inspired me to create a series of science fiction sketches that I still have today. Once I started to look into pursuing a career in entertainment, I was able to get an interview at Industrial Light & Magic in the Bay Area, George Lucas's visual effects company. Since I was not a computer engineer (those were the only people working with computers at that time), they suggested I go to Hollywood where all the live-action production was happening. From that point on, I knew I was destined for Hollywood. I started buying books on topics like screenwriting, getting an agent, making your own short films—everything I could get my hands on that would teach me how to get into "the business." One of the books—the one about making your own short—basically came out and said something along the lines of, "You can pay to go to film school, or you can take that money and make your own film. You'll learn either way." And that was a light-bulb moment for me. *I can just make my own film.* Video had started evolving at that time, so some movies were being made on video for a lot less. It was just a matter of having a decent script and getting people together to make it happen.

At one point, I resorted to selling Winnebago motorhomes, so I had a little money from that brief gig. I borrowed the rest from my dad and stepmom. I wrote, produced, and directed a short film that eventually made it into Sacramento's local film festival, the 1996 Festival of Cinema. I dragged a bunch of my friends and family out to the screening at the United Artists theater downtown, bursting with pride. *I made this,* I told myself. *I completed something. I created a new story.* And by doing that, by telling a new story, I realized I might be able to change the old ones too.

With a completed film under my belt, I knew that there was only one place I could go: I packed up and moved to Los Angeles. I knew no one there, but I was confident. I got a job waiting tables and I started going to auditions, doing my stand-up at night at the Improv and the Comedy Store, and writing as many scripts as I could manage. Some of the friends I made from that time got pretty famous and had some tremendous success, people like Mark Curry, John Henton, Brian Posehn, Patton Oswalt, Greg Behrendt, and Carlos Alazraqui. I was stoked for them. They inspired me and showed me what was attainable as a creative soul.

In 1998 I got my first real "Hollywood" job working for a guy named Seth Epstein. Seth was a visionary who had a very hip and successful production company called FUEL. Everyone wanted to work there. I started out as a lowly production assistant and slowly worked my way up to production coordinator, then production manager. Seth was the guy who introduced me to *The Secret,* and the Law of Attraction as it relates to really focusing on what you want as opposed to what you don't want. In *The Secret,* author Rhonda Byrne talks about three concepts that are key to the Law of Attraction: Ask, Believe, and Receive. He taught me how to ask for what I want, believe I deserve it, and then be open to receiving it. Seth saw the talent and the good in me. Because of Seth, I started to see that by believing I was a capable person, able to accomplish whatever I set my heart to, I truly became that person. I leaned into my desires—imagined them becoming a part of my future—and let those wants drive my work, the effort that would bring them to fruition. The same went for believing that I was healthy, and that I was lovable. I never abandoned my program, but *believing* that I was sober made sobriety that much simpler. Seth's approach to money fell into that category too.

My mom had grown up on a ranch during the Depression, so her understanding of money was colored by her experience of scarcity and want. "Money doesn't grow on trees," she'd tell us. Because my mom seemed to come from a place of fear, I grew up thinking that the people who had money were innately evil. The only way they could have gotten that money, I reasoned, was by taking it from other people. This internal reasoning flew in the face of my own experience. As a child, I'd had a paper route in a wealthy neighborhood, and as I went door to door, collecting for the paper, I met lovely, kind people, like Sam and Sharon Anapolsky, who had a big, beautiful home, a swimming pool and enough money to send their kids, Bruce and Jill, to nice schools. The Anapolskys were very good to me, inviting me in during the holidays and appreciating and respecting me throughout the rest of the year. Bruce and Gayla Mace were also very kind and supportive of my art very early on.

The fear that my mom had drilled into me, like her anxiety about money, had no foundation in reality. I do think that her life experience—my dad leaving her to fend for herself with seven kids while he went off and built a nice, affluent life for himself—must have contributed to her outlook. We struggled with money for years, and to see my dad doing well for himself and taking virtually no notice of us . . . that must have had a terrible effect on the way my mom thought about wealth and the people who have money. And she inadvertently passed that suspicion and resentment on to me.

But Seth's approach to money was entirely different. He showed me that the Law of Attraction had some pretty strong legs under it, particularly when it came to thinking about money and being open to receiving it. Ever since I changed my perspective on taking care of my finances, I've never had to worry about money. And that's something that can benefit everyone. We've all got champagne appetites and beer incomes, and if you're still living an addiction-based life, you're going to end up blowing your money. One of my mentors, an amazing guy named Milton Dicus, taught me that the easiest way to get out of that cycle is to save 10 percent of everything you make and then live below the means of whatever you've got left over.

As an organizing principle, it's really simple. If you live even a little below what's left of your means, you're saving that much more. Everyone struggles with money—God knows I've had my own problems in that area—but the answer is surprisingly simple. A change in attitude will do wonders. Change the story. That's why I have a sign on my vision board that reads, "Money Comes Easily and Frequently."

But Seth did more for me than just introduce me to a better way of thinking about money. He taught me about being impeccable with my word, the first of Don Miguel Ruiz's Four Agreements. That agreement includes always speaking in the direction of truth and love, and never speaking unkindly about yourself or others. It recognizes the power of the positive spoken word. Seth was the one who helped me put visualization into practice, and encouraged me to work to become an executive producer at Charlie Company. I told you earlier that I'd photoshopped my name onto an executive producer business card; that was for Chris Pagani and Ryan Riccio at Charlie Company. I took that business card and stuck it to the door of my bedroom, and three months later, I had that exact job. That was the first time I realized how powerful visualization can be.

And this is the reality of shoveling coal. Sure, a big part of it is the day-to-day stuff: showing up to work on time, being prepared, putting in the effort to do a good job, doing what you say you are going to do when you say you are going to do it, and keeping your relationships respectful and kind . . . but another big part of it is the empowerment that comes from taking responsibility for yourself.

I didn't understand this part of it for a long time. My brother Paul—an amazing doctor and all-around fantastic human being—used to come home from college and see how I was struggling with our stepfamily, all that fighting and misery and anger and helplessness. He'd take me aside and try to talk to me.

"You're in control, man," he'd say. "You're in control."

Every time this happened, it just made me angrier. But it was the truth.

"I'm not in control," I'd tell him, fuming. "That's the problem. Mom and Cass [my stepdad] have all the power. They're calling the shots. They're forcing me to go to basketball practice just because my stepbrother plays basketball. I don't want to play basketball! They're the ones in control."

It took me a lifetime to realize that my brother wasn't talking about the argument. He knew who had the authority in the situation, whether it was a fight over basketball practice or whether I could stay out past nine on a Friday night. He knew it wasn't me. But he also knew that I wasn't in control of *myself*, and that lack of control was at the root of all these conflicts. What I've learned, through a hard-won life of shoveling coal, is that taking responsibility for yourself is the only way to achieve power over the rest of your life. It is the key to happiness.

You have to do it yourself. You have to exercise control over your own attitude and actions, and once you've got that in hand, once you're sure that your perspective is one that will not only let you see the situation clearly, but also help you make healthy choices and find the best path forward, every facet of your life gets better . . . and the story begins to change.

CHAPTER 3

The Passenger Car

AUGHTER. THE QUIET RUSTLE OF a newspaper. As you enter the Passenger Car, you're struck by the sudden shift in tone. Whereas the Coal Car was all fire and soot and the roar of the engine just beyond the heat of the furnace, the Passenger Car feels quiet, almost civilized. Gently presented men and women sit in rows, reading or listening to music or talking quietly, and as you pass each row, you realize that every face is familiar to you. There is your little brother. Your sister. An old boyfriend.

We carry our people with us. Not the actual people (not even in this extended metaphor), as we all have our own trains to run, but our personal representations of them, built on memory and colored with emotion. Those representations change with every year that passes; as our perspective changes over time, so do the representations of the people we carry with us.

A wise man once told me, "Your children are your passengers, and you are the passenger of your children." Setting aside the real-world implications of familial care, his point is that there is no escaping your history. Wherever you go, you bring your people with you. They will always be a part of you.

I have reason to regret this fact, but a child's memory is not perfect. I know that the representations I have of my mother and father and stepparents are not totally accurate. That is to say, I can rely on my memories of what happened and the stories that were told to me, but I cannot accurately ascribe motivations to the various players. All I can do is recount as many of the facts as I can remember and try to apply the perspective of age to this somewhat fraught subject.

I wasn't just the youngest of the original seven; I was the youngest by a mile, and I don't believe my arrival was expected. Right after I was born, my clever, well-spoken father left my mother to care for all of us on her own. When I was little, it felt like it was just my mom and me because my sister, who was my next oldest sibling, is six years my senior. She was out with cousins and friends much of the time, so I received the bulk of my mom's attention, and I flourished. When I look at pictures of myself during that time, I look happy and I have very fond memories of that period of my youth. I painted and drew, and she taught me to love nature and stories. But then, when she remarried, this time to a man with five children of his own, four kids moved into my bedroom. Four new brothers—if you can call them that. As far as I was concerned, they were just four threatening strangers who were bigger than me, four boys who suddenly moved into my bedroom and gained all the intimate access to my life and my person that they wanted.

It was the start of some really tough times. From the age of seven until fourteen, I was molested multiple times by several older male and female family members. Being sexualized as a child was the cause of much subsequent shame and confusion that would last well into adulthood. These were deep, dark secrets that haunted me for decades and led to excruciating self-hatred. In most of my adult relationships, I confused love with sex and pity. I had no capacity for true intimacy. I was never able to talk about any of this until I was in therapy in my fiftieth year.

And when it came to those new siblings in particular, I had nowhere to hide. My stepfather wasn't someone I ever felt I could turn to. From the beginning, it was clear that I didn't like him, and he didn't like me. So I grew angrier. I went from being a bright, happy little kid to a ball of raw nerves and anger. From the time I was seven until my mom and stepfather kicked me out of the house, I was constantly angry and perpetually frightened. I began to fight with everyone. My new stepbrothers. My new stepfather. Everyone who represented the loss of my mother's attention was fair game in the roulette of my rage.

When you merge two families—one with six boys and one girl, the other with four boys and one girl—the predictable result is chaos. Worse than chaos, it was pandemonium. Some of the older kids started drinking alcohol, smoking pot, and dropping acid. One of my brothers even hopped a few freight trains and we thought he was going to end up a hobo. It was easy to get lost in the shuffle, and there was no time for thoughtful parenting, so my mother and stepfather instead opted for corporal punishment. It was a different time.

I remember one time my sister had been picking on me, so I wrecked her bicycle and hid it in the bushes. My brother Paul sometimes felt compelled to play peacemaker, so he came to me in the dorm, the room where all the boys slept, and coaxed the story from me. When I told him, he swore he wouldn't say anything to our mother, but he immediately went to tell her, because what seemed like only seconds later, my mom came flying into the dorm with a thick, leather cowboy belt. She screamed at me and whipped me until welts appeared on the backs and tops of my thighs. The next day in physical education class, I kept having to pull my blue nylon shorts lower to hide the black-and-blue strap marks.

I know my mother loves me. She always has. I also know now that this was physical abuse, that my mother had no right to beat me, and that if I were a child now, there are structures in place to protect me from that kind of mistreatment. But at the time, I had no one to turn to. In my view, the mother I'd adored had been replaced by this overworked and spiteful person who thought that beating me would save her time and let her get on to dealing with the next problem.

It didn't help matters that I believed my family blamed me for my father's departure. My mother would never say so, but the fact that I was born six years after my sister suggested to me that I was not part of the original plan for the family—and the portraits that hung in the dining room said it loud and clear.

The dining room was the central room of the house. You had to walk through it to get from the bedrooms to the kitchen; every day, back and forth, it was a thoroughfare for the whole family. On the dining room wall were a pair of picture frames, each with three inset oval photos: one baby picture of each of my siblings . . . but not one of me. My family never thought to add my baby picture to the wall, not in the two decades I lived in that house.

I don't know why this happened. The part of me that wants to rationalize, to leap to my family's defense, says that an unexpected kid is a lot to cope with, and my parents were already pretty overwhelmed, and what does a baby picture on the wall really mean, anyway?

And then I remember that I asked about this conspicuous absence several times, and after my stepsiblings moved into the house, they noticed too, and taunted me about it whenever they wanted to hurt me. There were a lot of us, I know, but hanging a picture on the wall would have been a small thing for my parents, and it would have meant so much to me. It would have meant that I was part of the family, that even though no one had expected my arrival, they still loved me and wanted me. They couldn't even do that, and it hurt. It wounded me deeply.

Plenty of other families expand suddenly and yet are still filled with love and laughter. And throughout the early part of my childhood, I'd thought I had that. Then my stepdad moved in, and everything changed for the worse.

Why did my home life turn so toxic? One explanation for my mom's souring could be that I must have reminded her of my father. He also struggled with the bottle, and the personal similarities between us have always been hard to ignore. When my mom was overwhelmed or just tired, she'd get in her cups and then take it out on me. I think she was so angry with my father for leaving that it became hard for her to even look at me without resenting me.

My stepfather wasn't any better. One evening I had gotten into some argument with my mother that had blown up beyond any reasonable sense of proportion—picture a small, cramped kitchen, made crowded by my brothers, their girlfriends, and the weight of a vicious verbal battle between my mom and me. My stepfather came in, saw that we were fighting, and clocked me. His fist hit me so hard that he knocked me out. I remember lying on the floor, hearing the buzz of voices around me, and being unable to get up or open my eyes. I don't know how long it took me to come to, but it wasn't a trivial amount of time.

Our house was loud and violent. My brother Bobby, the second oldest, wrote a poem, "Through Barely a Window," about our family. He wrote of a brutal fight he witnessed in the house between my father and my Uncle Richard while I was still an infant. When you're a kid, that kind of atmosphere is deeply damaging. I remember riding my bicycle home from school one afternoon, slowing as I rode down Burbank Way, and wanting to ride right past my driveway. Every time I came home, I had to mentally prepare myself for the potential chaos inside. Who should I ally myself? Who should I stay the hell away from? Who is drunk? Who is high? Who is going to throw a plate at dinner? Every day, these questions had different answers.

And then, at the age of twelve, I discovered alcohol. I was at my grandmother Edna's birthday party, and I found out where the champagne was hidden. My cousin and I sneaked back into the kitchen and I started guzzling the bubbly. I drank myself into a blackout. Apparently, my aunt and cousins were trying to sober me up with coffee and a cold shower, to no avail. I woke up the next day to my mom smacking me because the phone was ringing off the hook. It was the neighbors calling because none of them had their morning newspaper, and, yes, I was the paper boy. I had slept through my alarm, or had never set it. At the age of twelve, alcohol had already started to affect my work. A sign of things to come.

Soon after, I discovered that if I mixed rum with Coke, I got Coke that made me happier. I started bringing the mixture with me to school and sharing it with my friends. Think about that for a moment. At the age when most kids are worrying about the social politics of junior high, I had drinking buddies. I am sure it led to me staying back in the eighth grade and having to repeat it at another new school.

A year later, I started sneaking down to the river with my buddies to smoke pot, and a year after that, I started snorting cocaine. By junior year, I was dealing it. Drugs most definitely played hell with my health, but they made me somewhat popular. I was a poor kid at a school for rich kids, and having access to drugs meant that lots of people wanted to hang out with me.

From the age of twelve, my life was marked by alcohol and drug abuse, and as much as I try to rationalize the way I was raised, the root of that drug use lay in my sense that my family had abandoned me. My father had left, and the superficial relationship we developed whenever Mom sent me to stay with him for the weekend was never strong enough to heal my resentment. My mom had abandoned me when she'd suddenly had to start taking care of all these new kids in addition to me. I know that stepchildren come with their own challenges, but knowing that she'd suddenly quintupled her workload didn't make her absence any easier for me to bear. I still had a mom-shaped hole in my life, and new, violent, aggressive stepbrothers could only fill that void with pain. When four stepbrothers moved into our house, it pushed my older brothers out into the newly built bunkhouse, and therefore, none of my real brothers remained close enough to protect me. Soon after, all my older brothers left for college, and that familiar feeling of abandonment was amplified. They'd never been great at protecting me from my stepsiblings, but any sense of safety vanished after they left.

I've been prone to feelings of abandonment for a long time, and I can trace them back to one particular incident. I was five or six at the time, so to cheer us up, my mom decided to take us all to Disneyland. She hadn't yet married my stepfather, so I believe it was just the eight of us—me, my mom, and six siblings—plus maybe an aunt and a couple of cousins. We'd all piled into the family station wagon, sleeping bags stacked to the ceiling, and headed south from Sacramento on Highway 99. Nowadays you'd take Interstate 5, but back then it hadn't been completed, and you had to go through a dozen little towns and hamlets before getting through Los Angeles and then to Anaheim. You'd stop in places like Bakersfield or Fresno to grab a bite to eat and fill up on gasoline.

The protocol for getting gas was very simple. You'd pull up at the pump, get the gas flowing, and let all the kids out to use the bathroom and the water fountain. Then you'd pile all the kids back into the car—in the "way back" we sat on bench seats, facing one another—and head out. Simple, right?

Not always. At some point during this trip, we pulled into a gas station in Turlock. We all got out to stretch our legs and use the toilet, or whatever, and then everyone got back into the car and the car drove off . . . everyone but me, that is. I was still in the bathroom when mom's station wagon turned back onto Highway 99. I came out of the bathroom, this tiny towheaded boy, surrounded by the vast, rural nothingness somewhere in the middle of Stanislaus County. The gas station attendant saw me, took a quick look around for people who might be my parents, and then fixed me with a look that I can only describe as, *Oh God, what am I going to do with this kid?*

My family didn't even realize I was missing. Apparently the gas station attendant had to call the highway patrol and get someone to track down my mom's Ford Country Squire behemoth, pull her over, and tell her that she'd forgotten one of her kids at the gas station at least twenty miles back. I sat with that attendant in the shade, using a big old oil drum for a card table, and he tried to teach me a card game while we waited for the station wagon to return.

Over the years I've been teased quite a bit about that incident. It's the funniest story anyone ever tells about me—the time I was forgotten at a gas station in Turlock. My family told the story over and over.

But it wasn't funny for me. I was terrified, and looking back on it, I was right to be frightened. Anything could have happened to me. That gas station attendant didn't have to be a good dude in that situation. He didn't have to call the highway patrol. He could have done anything to me, and no one would've been the wiser. But more frightening than that for me was the sudden, icy realization that my family could forget about me. That I wasn't loved enough for anyone to keep track of me. They could lose me at any time and not think twice about it.

From that incident, I learned that I had to look out for myself, that the people I was supposed to trust couldn't be relied upon. That pattern held true for the rest of the time I lived with my family. I had days when someone was supposed to come pick me up from school and no one came; I'd sit next to my teachers while we waited for them, and listen to them wondering aloud, "Who forgets their kid?" Sometimes my mom would forget me at the grocery store even though I was the only kid who'd come with her. It didn't help that everyone tried to brush these incidents off as cute, funny anecdotes: "Our family is so big and wild that sometimes we forget the littlest one even exists." Ha ha.

Again and again, the "story" I got from my family: you don't matter.

Sometimes it's hard to remember that just as you've got representations of all the people in your life buzzing around in your Passenger Car, they each have a representation of you living in theirs. I'm sure that there is an objectively true version of what happened in those moments when I was left at that gas station. But I have only my memories and their stories to rely on, just like everyone else in my family. They've downplayed the incident for so long that to them it is nothing more than a funny footnote in our collective history. I know that certain events happened: a police car was there, and I waited long enough to watch that gas station attendant get through more than a few games of solitaire—even if my siblings deny it. Even if they've convinced themselves that it wasn't as bad as I remember, and that the memory of a six-year-old is not to be trusted. We're all dealing with the straw-man representations of one another that we've installed in our Passenger Cars. More importantly, it's the story created from a single perspective.

This is exactly why the stories we tell ourselves matter so much. The world has its own version of your story, and if you accept it as your own, you're allowing yourself to be ruled by that version. I learned from an early age that I didn't matter and could be safely forgotten. This was a lie—a deeply destructive lie. And it led to an incredibly destructive history of drug use, alcoholism, and self-harm.

So how did I escape that lie? A huge component of that escape was my late, great mentor and my greatest teacher,

Bob Palmer. Bob was the father I'd never had. He was the father figure I'd always needed. I've said for a long time that if I could design my own father and then mash him up with the Buddha, I'd end up with Bob.

A lot of people tried to talk to me about my suicide attempt, partly because it was clearly a symptom of a much larger problem, and partly because even after I got into recovery, I was still incredibly depressed. I fantasized a lot about suicide, about doing it right, for once. It felt like the easiest path. I could just pull a trigger or hang myself. Suicide seemed so easy. But Bob finally destroyed that fantasy with the power of the spoken word.

"James," he said to me, "what if when you killed yourself, the pain didn't go away?"

That stopped me in my tracks. He let me ponder that for a while.

Then he continued, "Or, what if, when you killed yourself, the pain just got worse?"

Wow. I had never heard anything like that before. It goes against my upbringing, but I've always believed in karma. Bob's questions forced me to reexamine my vision of the afterlife. My friend Kevin says, "Shortcuts are the quickest way to the back of the line." Well, because of what Bob said to me that day, I came to the conclusion that if the karmic circle is real, then suicide is that shortcut. It's the quickest way to the back of the line. You're going to come back, and you're going to have to do all of this all over again. You've still got to learn those missing lessons, feel those unfelt feelings.

But Bob's wisdom extended far beyond pulling me away from the edge of darkness. He was the person who taught me I was telling myself these "stories." He made me look at them and reevaluate the stories I was telling myself. He'd heard me talk about how unlovable I was, about what a disappointment I was to my parents, and how they neglected me because nothing about me was worthy of their time. He gave me permission to change my stories and to create new ones. And he said something so gentle, so loving, that I'll never forget it. He would repeat it to me when I was being hard on myself: "Be on your own side. Be on your own side, kid." I think of this any time I am pushing myself too hard. I hear his gentle, loving voice say, "Be on your own side, kid."

I'd never realized that in the conflict between my parents and me, it was possible for my side to be worth choosing. I didn't know that I could choose myself. I didn't know how.

That epiphany enabled me to recognize that the people I'd imagined my family to be were imaginary representations. They weren't absolutely true, just like the stories they'd told me about myself weren't absolutely true. I started to look at what is good about my family members today. I started to focus on the good times. I started to believe that I am worthy. I am lovable. And recognizing that it's possible to believe a lie you've told yourself, whether it's about the people in your life or the way you see yourself, is the first step toward changing your story.

CHAPTER 4
The Baggage Car

I T'S DARK IN THE BAGGAGE Car. There is none of the soft
lighting that kept the Passenger Car feeling clean and cozy.
Just a naked bulb overhead, flickering, swaying as the train
rounds a bend. The steel walls are thin, and the rumble of the
train is almost deafening. And there's a dank smell. Hard to
place, but faintly musty, like old cedar blocks. It's hard to be
in this car, as if the mounds of crates and bags and traveling
chests know you're looking at them and resent you for it.

The longer you spend here, the better your eyes acclimate,
until seeing through the gloom is almost easy. Comfortable.
Everywhere, baggage is piled to the ceiling, each piece labeled
in your own handwriting. "Mistakes," read a few. Bags piled
in the corner of the car all read "Regrets," and here and there
amid the rubble you find labels with little subtitles: "The Girl

I Never Asked Out," "The Time I Misjudged My Brother," and "Cruel Insults I Used When I Felt Inadequate." You step deeper into the car, your hand trailing along buckles and zippers and faux leather, until your gaze stops on the piles in the very back of the car, furthest from the door, shrouded in deepest shadow. One is marked "Abuse." Another says "Trauma." One reads "Molestation." Your feet seem cemented in place. There is no forward movement now. Perhaps you can back up and return to happier memories? But no. You are riveted, unable to turn away, frozen by these naked horrors.

We've all lived through angst and hardship. We all carry baggage that weighs us down, that slows our train. Many of us deal with this baggage by shoving it into the darkest recesses of our memories, only to have it reemerge during moments of joy or triumph. Carrying this weight, these old painful stories can poison our lives. It's only by pausing at way stations, opening the car and airing it out, and ultimately unloading this terrible freight (i.e., by relying on a community of genuine and supportive peers) that we can clean out our Baggage Cars and push forward along the tracks that lie ahead of us.

What weight are you carrying? What's your "story"?

For decades, I carried around a grief that I could never express.

When I was nineteen, I waited tables at Leatherby's, a local ice cream parlor owned by some family friends, and that's where I first saw this cute little blonde, blue-eyed, darling of a girl,

Vicki Johnson. She was dating a guy named Al, whom she'd been seeing since high school. A nice guy, he would drop by work occasionally to see her. Their relationship slowly changed and Vicki started to share with me her desire to get out and experience "more." I had always been smitten with Vicki but had respected her relationship with Al.

We had a great group of coworkers and we all got on really well together—either because we'd bonded in the kind of solidarity that occurs in a service business, or because there was something about our group that just kind of clicked. We had each other's backs. We kept each other honest. So when I started noticing cracks in Vicki and Al's relationship, I tried to be there for her. Vicki and I grew closer—I loved her sweetness and her surprisingly wicked sense of humor—and she and Al eventually drifted further apart.

I started to spend more time with Vicki, and that was really the only thing I wanted. We started dating, and I remember those days being happier and more carefree than any of the days I'd had since my mom had remarried. It was like I'd struck gold. All things were possible. She was an absolute angel.

One Saturday night, after a date, we were hanging out at my good friend Alan Hammond's apartment. It was getting late, and she decided to head home. I kissed her good night. She got in her little white Mustang and drove off. We didn't see each other that Sunday; she had to work, and I had the day off. But we shared the Monday morning lunch shift, and I was looking forward to seeing her then.

That Monday, I showed up at the restaurant as usual, and our boss called me into the office. He sat me down and explained that the night before, Vicki had been killed in a drunk-driving accident. Vicki and several of our coworkers had gotten together and were drinking beers. A bunch of us rode motorcycles, and one of the guys was showing off his new bike and giving rides to anyone who would get on. Vicki, being the adventurous young woman she was, climbed onto the back.

The strangest thing was that I couldn't seem to react to the news. At all. I sat there, stunned, not crying, not really feeling anything other than confusion. None of it made any sense. None of it felt real. I thought perhaps I ought to cry, that I ought to feel *something*—but nothing happened. After some time, I decided to go for a ride, so I got on my motorcycle and I rode to Winding Way, the place where she'd died, a telephone pole at the wrong place on a sharp curve. He must have been going too fast. He must have hit a rock or something. Spun out. Hit the telephone pole.

I still couldn't cry.

I rode over to her folks' place, intruding on their own grief, and I sat on her bed in her room and looked around at her unicorns and her glass figurines—all the stuff of her childhood, still on display—and I still couldn't cry. But I didn't want to leave. I ended up asking her folks if there was anything I could do for them, and they let me clean their above-ground pool. But it didn't help. I still couldn't feel the loss.

The funeral was five days later. I rode my motorcycle there and sat at the back of the chapel and shut down. Not crying. Not talking. Not doing anything. I just shut down.

I kept that shutdown going for years, but the pain that caused it—whether I could engage it or not—stuck. Looking back, I now realize I drank at that pain, that final abandonment, for the next five years.

Some things never leave you. One year—I was probably four or five—my mom was dating I guy I knew as Mr. McKenna. He was all in on the family, and he and his children loved me. That was pretty clear. He took me to a football game in South Lake Tahoe for my birthday and gave me three different Tonka trucks—which, as you can imagine, was like winning the lottery for a four-year-old. For kids, in particular, presents feel like tangible demonstrations of intangible concepts. Because Mr. McKenna had given me those Tonka trucks, I felt loved and safe and cared for, in a way that went far beyond someone telling me that they loved me.

But it couldn't last. Mom stopped seeing him and eventually married my stepfather, and then money got really tight. With twelve kids, it was inevitable. We were told that we all had to do our part and help out. So we all got paper routes, and we all started going door to door collecting cans, bottles, and newspapers from the neighbors to turn in for much-needed cash. It was incredibly humiliating to go from being happy, cared for, and content to having to announce our new poverty to our neighbors and our schoolmates. Before I was born, when my dad bought our house, we'd had a corral, stables, a little red barn, and horses, but after he left, that all had to go. The stables were torn down to build a bunkhouse for the older boys, and the corral was tilled and repurposed into a large vegetable garden. We didn't have much money for groceries, so we fed ourselves out of the garden: corn, tomatoes, swiss chard, carrots, squash, and zucchini. We had some fruit trees, and Mom would make preserves from the plums and apricots and peaches. From a modern perspective, all that living off the land sounds kind of idyllic, but the reality is that while it's nice to have fresh fruits and veggies from your own garden, the shine wears off the minute it becomes the only food you can afford.

My birthdays became drab, dismal affairs. It seemed there was no money for presents, and definitely no money for a party. So I watched as my schoolmates celebrated their own special days with blowout parties and entertainers. One year my dad forgot my birthday and tried to make it up to me the day after. After a while, even pointing out my birthday became a disappointment, the kind of thing that just hurt me at the core and made me sad. I stopped thinking about celebrations pretty quickly after my stepfamily moved in. No sense in reopening old wounds.

Flash forward to today: I have a life beyond my wildest dreams, money isn't a problem, and love isn't a problem. My beautiful, loving partner, Elisabeth, wants to know what I want for Christmas. And I can't go there. Receiving gifts feels so tainted—forbidden to me, even—that every time she asks, I mumble something about being blessed and having more than I need, and I hope she'll just drop it. But she doesn't. She's generous and kind, and she loves me and wants to give me nice things. So finally, after the last time she asked, and the last time I dodged the question with furtive denials and weak assertions that everything was fine, she threw my own words right back at me: "If you say so." Ouch.

And suddenly I knew what I was doing. I was telling myself that my past was painful, and that story was letting my past taint my present. I was hanging on to that story, that leftover from my childhood, when presents really did matter and they never came, and I was acting as though I still had that life. I was telling myself that I was still that little boy.

It was up to me to change this. So I sat down and wrote out a Christmas list. Nothing extravagant. Nothing pie-in-the-sky or undoable. Just a list of some things I was thinking about maybe getting for myself, but didn't feel like I could justify quite yet. I gave her that list, and come Christmas morning, all of those things, and more, were under the tree. And it was nice—really nice. I felt loved and safe and cared for in a way I hadn't since Mr. McKenna gave me those Tonka trucks.

I still feel a little uncomfortable when receiving gifts. Poverty leaves deep marks on you, after all. But I don't court that feeling of unworthiness, and I certainly don't let it dictate the way I live my life. If someone gives me a present, I am gracious, I say thank you, and I let myself feel loved.

But some trauma isn't so easily left behind. Sometimes it sticks with you and reemerges at the worst moments.

There was a day, a few years after my stepfather moved in, when I learned one of the defining lessons of my childhood. I had been skateboarding at a friend's house, and he'd shot some footage and then sent it off to have it developed. The day it came back, half a dozen of us kids were eager to see it. Our skateboarding tricks, captured on film. Nothing could be cooler. My friend's dad had a film projector, and there was a big blank wall in my friend's bedroom, perfect for a viewing party. We all filed in, leaving our skateboards outside, careful to respect this house that would host one of the coolest things we ever expected to see. My friend turned out the lights and got the footage rolling.

That was when I felt a hand on my thigh.

As we'd entered the house, my friend's next-door neighbor—not a kid, but a grown man, hulking and balding—had followed us in. I'd even seen him come in with us, scraping his loafers on the doormat. I'd just assumed that he was invited, somehow. That he was meant to be there. But as I sat on my friend's bed in the dark, surrounded by my skating friends, this man slowly slid his hand up my thigh, reached into my shorts and began to fondle my genitals. I was in shock. I froze.

In the dark I silently grabbed his hand and threw it away from me, and then I ran out the door and raced home, doubtless leaving my friends in deep confusion. I told my mom, and I don't think it sank in at first. Her reaction was more puzzled than angry, and that should have been what tipped me off that this wasn't going to go well. She brought my stepfather into the conversation when he got home from work, and instead of being enraged, they both started to act awkward. Looking back, the awkwardness was too much even for me—I downplayed the events, saying that he may have "dragged his fingers across" my crotch instead of the much more accurate terminology I've used here. But I can't blame myself. I was terrified—of my stepfather, of what my friends would say, of what *their* parents would say. Something terrible had happened to me, and I was immediately concerned about the social fallout.

My mother and stepfather did the right thing, and called my friend's parents and organized a meeting at the house where the incident had occurred. The kids who were there joined the meeting, along with their parents. I did my best to explain in front of everyone what had happened. I remember how awkward it was. All eyes and ears were on me. Grown men were questioning me over and over. It was very difficult; I felt like I was making trouble, just creating a headache for them.

Eventually, my friend's father, a prominent dentist in town—I think in order to avoid liability—tried to downplay what had happened to me. He and the other men pointed out that if they were to approach this man and accuse him of touching me inappropriately, he would most likely just deny it. It would be a grown man's word against the word of a confused eleven-year-old. So, the decision was made.

They all, including my parents, decided to do nothing.

I don't know how they justified it to themselves. I know they weren't alone, though. I kept this stuffed down inside for decades. It wasn't until I turned fifty that I was able to talk about it in therapy, where I was also able to finally talk about the other molestations that had occurred as well. It was triggered after the Jerry Sandusky case came out at Penn State. I realized my parents were like Joe Paterno: they knew, and they did nothing. I knew then that this man was a predator, and no one had tried to stop him.

I learned from my parents' inaction that I was essentially alone. The story that came out of that experience was that no one else was going to protect me, not ever. I couldn't rely on anyone except myself. As I grew up, that conviction never left me. I grew into a kid who was constantly at odds with his own family. I was constantly coming home drunk and high. My folks caught me with drugs and alcohol; they came home to me fighting with my brothers, breaking doors in the house, punching holes in the drywall, and throwing knives at a target on the back of my bedroom door. It got so my mom was afraid to open the door to my bedroom, which was exactly what I wanted. If I was truly alone, if it was really me against the world, then what right did my mom have to try to control me?

I knew I wasn't the only victim of life's cruel circumstances; I saw their impact everywhere I looked. When I had my paper route, copies of the *Sacramento Bee* would arrive on our porch before sunrise, and I would sit on the cold floor of the family room, folding them for delivery. Alone in the dark, the headlines seemed to jump off the page, especially those about the East Area Rapist—a man who would prowl the quiet neighborhoods of Sacramento, looking for women who lived alone and were vulnerable. He would follow them weeks in advance to learn their routines and plot his attacks. He'd break in when they weren't home to unlock windows and doors and plant the tools he'd need later—such as ligatures to tie them up with—and eventually return to ransack their homes and their bodies and ruin their lives. I must have seen thirty or forty headlines about the East Area Rapist striking again and again.

Everything seemed to change during that time. I had two older teenage sisters, Patricia and Laurie, and we all feared for their safety. We stopped leaving our doors unlocked and added extra latches. As we watched and waited with bated breath, any innocence I had left eroded. I learned that the world was a cruel place and anything could happen to any of us at any time, and I couldn't do anything to stop it; no one could.

I maintained that attitude for a very long time, deep into my sobriety. But an essential part of a successful sobriety program is making an effort to help other people along their path, even if this puts you at odds with your own personal philosophy. At one point I committed to volunteering at Folsom State Prison, knowing that the men there needed just as much help in healing as I did, if not more. Once a month on Sunday mornings, I'd drive out to the prison, get through the screening process, and then be marched out past the large cafeteria where there were conjugal visits. We would head back deep into the prison and down the stairs next to the yard, where the prisoners were all playing basketball and lifting weights, and into the tiny law library that was there for the inmates. It was in that library that we held our groups. As volunteers, we would be left there with no guard in the room until the group was finished.

The gatherings were small, usually 75 percent black, 25 percent Latino, and the energy in the room was tense, at least for me. It was a scary place to be, but I trusted God and the work that I was doing. One morning, the day after I'd just broken up with a girlfriend, a few of the guys were being disruptive.

I'd brought a couple of older guys from my home group along to speak, hoping that their age and serious demeanor could finally get through to these guys, but the inmates weren't having it. They chatted with one another, snickering and joking around, heedless of the things my friends were saying. I realized that I didn't have the patience for their rowdiness anymore. I finally snapped.

When it was my turn to speak, I said, "You know what? No one pays us to come here. These two gentlemen got up early and left their families behind specifically so they could come out here and share their experiences with you. It's not cool, the way you're carrying on. Talking while they are trying to help you, and playing grab-ass."

I knew that I was surrounded by hardened criminals, but it didn't matter. This was material that had literally saved my life. I believed in it like nothing else, and dammit, these guys needed to respect what we were doing. I was tired and beyond caring, and my girlfriend was gone. And I was alone. Again. Brokenhearted, I was on the verge of tears anyway, and I was going to speak my mind. The two older men I had brought were looking at me like, *What the fuck are you doing?* and it didn't matter to me at all.

I said to the room, "My heart's been torn out already this week. And we still came to help you. We love you guys, and we're trying to help. You've got to respect that."

And in that moment, the body language of the room shifted. All these men were now focused on me and they weren't happy I was calling them out. A man I had come to know over several visits, named Ali—a huge, barrel-chested man, at least six feet six, with hands that could tear a phone book in half—leaned forward into the circle. The men leaned back, like the Red Sea parting, and the whole room went quiet.

"Let me get this straight," he said, his voice like an earthquake. "You come into my house, you and your old, white men; you come on your own accord, on your own time, nobody getting paid, trying to help us out, and all you want is for us to respect the things you say?"

I squeaked out a "Yeah."

He stared me down, looked at the men I brought in, paused, and without taking his eyes off of us, said in his deep voice, "All right, gentlemen. We're going to respect these men when they come here." He just laid down the law. His word was final.

And it was. From that point on, the guys listened and started to get involved and started asking questions about the materials, really participating.

At the end of the meeting, as we waited for the inmates to go back into the prison, Ali came over to me.

"Stand up, little one," he said (that's what he called me), and when I did, he wrapped his huge, tree-branch arms around me, enveloping me in this vast ocean of a hug. I was so frail, but I'd never felt safer than I did in that moment. It was ironic that one of the safest places I have ever stood on this earth was in Folsom Prison, maximum security, cellblock C, in a massive man's arms.

I found out later that Ali was in prison for murder—life without parole. But it didn't matter. I was safe with him because he'd seen the vulnerability in me, the deep-seated loneliness and the fatigue that come with feeling constantly alone, and he'd protected me from it. He was a spiritual man. He'd heard my truth. He'd connected with what I needed, and he'd given it to me. I knew, in that moment, that it was possible that I wasn't alone. That the story I'd been telling about only being able to rely on myself was maybe wrong, and there was a new possibility ahead. Maybe there were people I could trust in the world.

Trauma has a long shelf life. As long as you're alive and trucking along, the trauma of your past can keep haunting you. If you don't deal with it, it'll freeze in the moment, and every time something happens to you, every time you get the slightest whiff of a situation feeling uncomfortably familiar, that trauma is going to pop up and snatch you back into your former self. Bob Hoffman, creator of the Hoffman Process,[*]

---

[*] The Hoffman Institute, "What Is the Hoffman Process?" https://www. hoffmaninstitute.org/the-process/.

talks a lot about this kind of emotional regression, and I've spent a fair amount of time incorporating his psychological perspective into the way I deal with trauma.

Sometimes, when I end up thinking about that terrible moment in the dark of my friend's bedroom, I emotionally regress into the mind-set of myself as an eleven-year-old, a little boy being victimized by a grown man. And from that moment on, the rest of the day is poisoned; I feel bad. The moment his hand slid up my thigh is the filter through which I see the rest of my life. But I can check in with myself: *How's your physical body? Unpack your mind, your thinking, your intellect. Acknowledge the great things your intellect has afforded you. Unpack your emotional self here. How old are you, emotionally, right now?*

And as if I'm speaking from deep hypnosis, I'll respond, *I feel like I am eleven.*

Thank your emotional self for all the care it's taken of you. And then I'll visualize myself growing up to the age I am now.

And I'll realize, quite quickly, *I'm a fifty-five-year-old man. I'm powerful and spry. No one is molesting me today. I'm fine. I can care for myself today.*

Every time I flash back to that bedroom, I grow myself up again, and every time, it happens just a little bit quicker.

And that applies to all the horror stories of my childhood. I can allow myself to feel the feelings. And I don't have to do it alone. Using this slow but steady process of working through my trauma, experience after experience, I acknowledge that while it wasn't all bad, the bad things were bad enough to affect the story I'd tell about myself. They were bad enough to change the person I thought I was. But I'm *not* that person. I'm someone who has a completely different story, one rooted in love, truth, and work, and the expectation that I'm in charge of my own destiny. Like my mentor Clay Tatum says, "We make our own weather today."

There's another powerful adage that comes to mind when I think about all I've been through: "Make adversity pay you back." There were plenty of occasions when I was a victim, but I chose to remain one in the years that followed. My drinking, my destructive behavior, and the slew of decisions I made that hurt others took me into the depths of dark canyons and along sharp, craggy ridges, and caught me up in seemingly endless roundabouts. But once I became an adult, I didn't have to stay there; I had the power, the control, the awareness to change my story and take back my life. You do too. And sometimes that starts with forgiveness.

I'm not saying that people shouldn't be held accountable for their actions—not at all. But sometimes, in our unwillingness to forgive, we keep ourselves stuck, prevent ourselves from moving on. Why? Forgiveness isn't really about letting the people who have hurt you off the hook; it's about letting *yourself* off the hook. It allows you to become free.

I hated the man who had molested me for so long. I hated him so much that, finally, I decided I would track him down. I wanted to hold him accountable. I wasn't sure what I'd do when I found him, but I wanted some closure. Some answers. Something.

Shortly after I began my search, I found out he was dead. Confronting him wasn't an option. I'd have to find another way to find freedom, and to do that, I'd have to interrogate my own assumptions.

That's part of what the Hoffman Process does. It takes you back with a series of expanding questions, not just about your own experience, but also about every aspect of the encounter—including, in some cases, the abuser's perspective. *If they were that kind of person—someone awful, evil—who were they when they were just a child? What must have happened to them to make them think that was OK?* You have to dig deep into compassion and look at the whole story, rather than just seeing your own victimhood.

It shows you that regardless of why that person who hurt you did it—whether someone had hurt them or whether they were born that broken—you can change *your* story going forward. The process helps you build those spiritual muscles to become strong enough to rise above it all.

You can decide whether to stay there and remain the victim, or to let yourself off the hook and move on with your life. But

I'll warn you: when you hold onto those resentments, when you refuse to forgive, that tension remains—though you may be the only one feeling it. That tension gets pushed into your soul, causing all kinds of damage, physical and emotional. You can live with that horrific event playing on repeat, letting it trap you forever, until it becomes your undoing, or you can find a way to move on and go be fucking amazing. The choice is yours.

Bob Palmer, my late, great mentor, talked a lot about "detaching with love." For a long time, I didn't know what this meant. But as I grew, and started changing the story I told about myself, I realized that the people around me weren't going through the same process. My mom and my dad both lived in ways that played havoc with life. They both affected me in deeply destructive ways. Max Ehrmann's poem "Desiderata" tells us to "Avoid loud and aggressive persons" . . . but what if those loud and aggressive persons are the people you grew up believing you loved more powerfully than anyone else in the world? I can't avoid Mom. She's my *mom*.

But Bob took a gentler route.

"You don't have to shun anybody," he told me. "You're not abandoning them. You're not turning your back on them. Sometimes you just need to detach with love."

More important, it's crucial to your healing. There will always be people who don't want you to break the mold. They'll want you to fall back into the role of codependency and continue to cosign their negativity. Why? Misery loves company. But it's really important that you don't join them. You have to avoid that negativity—and the gossip and criticism that are often part and parcel of it. And you can do it with love.

It's not, "You're an evil, destructive influence, so I can't be around you ever again." It's as simple as, "I love you, but I'm gonna go over here. Not because you're dangerous, and not because I'm angry, but because you're not being kind. You hurt me, and you hurt the other people around you, and I'm not going to be party to that."

I love this idea. I love the idea that you can give yourself permission to "detach with love." The wording is so specific, so freeing and fulfilling, that it truly grants you power over your half of a relationship. It lets you free yourself from unhealthy relationships that don't serve you, and it lets you do that without abandoning the people you'll always care for.

And the thing is, it's not just people you can detach from. The more I engage with my baggage and the stories I've told myself, the better able I am to see which ones are healthy and which ones exist just to damage me. And at this point, I am able to recognize the truth of what happened to me—that I was molested as a child, and that none of my authority figures came to my aid—and detach from it. It's real, and it happened, but it doesn't need to be part of my life anymore. In letting go of that baggage, I can regain control.

Back when the East Area Rapist was terrorizing Sacramento, I had a close friend named Margaret Wardlow, whom I had known since kindergarten. She lived across Huntington Road, just a few houses down from mine. We used to run around the neighborhood unsupervised, building forts, climbing trees, running through fields, feeding the horses. But one day, when we were twelve or thirteen, something changed. All of a sudden, I didn't go over to her house anymore. I never really remember seeing her again. Our friendship was never the same, and no one ever told me what had happened.

Decades later, in 2017, my sister Patricia sent me an article about Margaret and how she had been the East Area Rapist's youngest victim at the age of thirteen.

"Weren't you friends?" Patricia asked.

"Yes," I replied, too stunned, hurt, sad, and confused to say anything more.

I went online and started researching. It was odd how many connections I had to the case. Sacramento's newly elected district attorney, Anne Marie Schubert, had been my classmate at St. Ignatius Grammar School in the '70s. Anne Marie herself had been very athletic and a pretty fierce competitor, and I knew Sacramento was in good hands with her. The East Area Rapist case had gone unsolved for decades, but she had renewed the city's commitment to it, releasing previous sketches and evidence that her predecessors had kept from the public. I saw and heard her determination, that fierce competitiveness that she had shown as a kid. It was reassuring to so many of us who lived in Sacramento and the surrounding area during those terrifying years.

The wife of my old friend Patton Oswalt, Michelle McNamara, a true-crime writer, was writing a book about the East Area Rapist who later became known as the "Golden State Killer" after he was connected to a series of murders throughout California. Tragically and unexpectedly, Michelle passed away before completing her book.

In 2018, someone called to inform me that Anne Marie had caught the Golden State Killer. A host of emotions flooded through me. It was surreal. I first thought of Margaret and hoped his capture offered her some relief, allowing her to heave some of that baggage from the depths of her Baggage Car. I thought of Patton and Michelle—how proud Michelle would have felt, and how the news must have lightened Patton's load a little. Patton was eventually able to posthumously release Michelle's book, *I'll Be Gone in the Dark: One Woman's Obsessive Search for the Golden State Killer.* I thought of Anne Marie, and how incredible it was that she never gave up. We all hope to make a difference in the world, and she had done something remarkable. She'd closed a cold case, helping so many people let go of some of the stuff weighing down their lives. She'd replaced the ellipsis on a long-unfinished story with a conclusion, and put an end to the fear that had haunted my siblings, my friends, and me as children and as adults. She'd set so many victims free.

That wasn't the only story with an ending that was a long time in the making. At the start of this chapter, I told you about the death of my sweetheart Vicki Johnson. For years, that was the whole story. I kissed my girlfriend good night, and the next day she was killed. But life is long, and that was never going to be the whole story.

Several years ago, I hit peak midlife crisis mode (I had just gotten divorced), so I bought a Harley-Davidson, a blue-and-white Softail Deluxe. She was beautiful and sleek. I bought her from an amazing, spiritual man, my friend Peter Ishkhans, who had named her Priscilla. I promptly took her on a long ride up to Northern California to see my family. As it happened, Peter regularly visited ashrams in India, and spent a lot of time meditating and doing yoga. When he sold Priscilla to me, I saw that he'd had "Namaste" printed on the gas tank in small, gentle gold letters. So as I rode, I found myself getting into a weirdly zen state of mind, until I was making navigational decisions based entirely on instinct. I call this "AI"—Actual Intelligence: "This left looks pretty good. This seems like the right kind of right," etc., without really knowing where I was going. And then, seemingly out of nowhere, it was right in front of me: Winding Way, where Vicki's accident had happened.

I rode down to the bend and stopped next to the telephone pole. Nearly thirty years after Vicki's accident, it's still there, though now there are flashing lights and guardrails—at least the county has figured out how dangerous the turn is—and the neighborhood seems to have gotten a little better. Otherwise, not much has changed. I pulled Priscilla off the road and stood there staring at the telephone pole. I glanced across the street to where an old man was gardening outside his house but keeping an eye on the noisy motorcyclist who had pulled up on a blind curve.

I gave him a gentle wave, and he returned it.

And then I asked, not really sure what I was expecting to happen, "Have you lived here long?"

He couldn't hear me, so he came across the street and I asked him again.

"I've lived here quite a while," he said.

So I said, still kind of numb, "Many years ago, my girlfriend was killed here on the back of a motorcycle with a buddy."

And this guy just looked at me.

He then put his hand on my shoulder and said, "I am the one who found them."

And it broke me. I lost it. I just started bawling. All those years of pent-up tears, all of those unfelt feelings. Looking around at her unicorns and figurines. Cleaning her parents' pool. Stone-faced at the back of the church. I let it all out.

I've lost so many people, and I'd been abandoned over and over again: My dad left us. My mom left me for my stepdad. My brothers left me at the mercy of our stepsiblings. And then Vicki left—forever. Game over. Something had clicked inside that day, some certainty that no one would ever hurt me again and no one would ever leave me again, and that certainty had shuttered my soul against the rest of the world.

And this man was the one who'd found Vicki. I told him everything I knew about her. How she'd loved unicorns. How she had been a high school cheerleader. He'd just been a man sitting at his kitchen table, and then he'd heard a terrible slam as the bike and its passengers hit the telephone pole.

"They died instantly," he told me. No pain. No lingering suffering.

I didn't think I was ready to hear it, not even that little detail. But it comforted me somewhat. And I think we both were able to heal a little.

CHAPTER 5

The Observation Car

AFTER THE NOISE OF THE Baggage Car, the roar and screech of the rails disconcertingly close, the quiet of the Observation Car comes as a shock. Here, the walls and floor seem padded, insulated against the sounds of machinery and the rushing wind. Your footsteps seem quieter, and you don't dare speak above a whisper. Part of that feeling comes from the brightness and airiness of the car, which is completely open with huge picture windows on either side. Sunlight streams in and pools in patterns on the floor, patterns that shift and ebb with every turn of the train.

You take a seat—on a low heap of soft cushions piled in a corner of the car, close enough to one of the windows that in the right light, you can see your reflection—and lose yourself in the landscape rushing past: green rolling hills, bustling townships, eerie forests, and great lakes. You see hikers and drivers and cyclists. You see arguments and reunions and people traveling together in companionable silence. And as day turns to night, you see the stars come out, distant and mysterious and yet somehow watchful. Welcoming.

This car is not a car for discovery, or for drama. It's not a car that must be battled or courted. In this car, everything is quiet and calm. There is no activity here, just gentle reflection upon the world as it slips by. It is your place on your train where your only purpose is to look out on the world, recognize that you are on your own path, and find a moment of peace.

A few years ago, I was filming segments for an action-sports network, focusing on skateboarding and surfing. Because I've always been passionate about these sports—I didn't grow up close to the ocean, so skateboarding was the next best thing to surfing for me—this job was right in my wheelhouse. Plus, it sent me to amazing places like Hawaii and Costa Rica, and more locally, to Santa Monica and Venice Beach—the mecca for surfing and skateboarding.

On this particular day, I was set to be in Trestles, in San Diego County, shooting footage of the Billabong Boost Mobile Pro surf contest. I'd had a dentist appointment that morning, so I wasn't able to get to the site until the crowds had already packed the beach, and the parking lot was jammed with cars. I parked way at the end, in the only empty spot I could find, and started the long slog through the parking lot, hauling my camera case and gear toward the beach. I passed car after car until I saw an SUV with its hatchback open. A guy was standing in the back working on his surfboards. That guy was Kelly Slater, eleven-time world champion, a giant in the surfing world. The true GOAT. To give you an idea, Tom Brady would have to win five more Super Bowls to do what Slater did. Slater had won all his heats the previous day, and he was taking his time getting down to the beach, as he wasn't surfing until early that afternoon.

He'd seen me before; if you film enough surfing footage, you can't help but look familiar to the pro surfers, so when I stopped, he recognized me. I asked him if he'd mind if I filmed him getting ready, and he said he didn't mind at all. So I unpacked my gear, set my camera up, and just started filming a bunch of detail work on Kelly Slater's prep process. It's not like I was there to shoot him—the world already had tons of Kelly Slater footage—but since I'd been hired to do a profile of a young, up-and-coming female surfer, Schuyler McFerran, it seemed like a good moment to see if I could get some words of wisdom out of this veteran surfer. So I started asking him questions. The best one I came up with—a clip that never made it into any videos, but which I still have and am proud of anyway—was this: "What's the single most important ingredient of competitive surfing?"

He was totally focused, in the zone, screwing in one of his fins, but he stopped, looked right into the camera lens, and said, "Patience." Then he went right back to tightening his fins. He knew the answer. It was simple. He didn't even have to think about it.

I've always been an impatient person, so his answer came as a bit of a shock—though it probably shouldn't have. You watch him surf, compared to the younger guys, and it's like night and day. The younger surfers are so anxious that they'll catch the first waves of a set, even if they're so small they're barely worth it. But Slater will wait for the bigger waves in the back. He'll sit, his legs dangling in the water, waiting patiently for a wave that is worth his time, and when it comes, he'll turn and paddle, drop in, and do five tricks on it all the way to the beach. His patience is one of the reasons why he's an eleven-time world champion. It's the thing that makes him great.

I've spent a lot of time trying to find something like Kelly Slater's powerful patience in myself. When I was young, my grandmother Edna used to make sure we never left the house without this reminder: "Remember who you are and what you represent." When she said it, I'm sure that she was telling us to mind our family history, to remember that our family spat out state senators and federal judges. Regal, august personages with unimpeachable reputations and names so bright and shiny they might as well have been gilded. *Remember that your family is noble*, she was telling us. *Don't do anything to tarnish the family name.* That's a lot to lay on a kid, particularly one who already feels like he doesn't fit in.

But as I got older, I started thinking about the literal meaning of her reminder: "who you are" and "what you represent." For an embarrassingly long time, I had little to no clue who I was. Sure, I knew my name, and I knew my history, and I knew all that stuff about my family—even the bit about how the governor of California came to my mom and dad's wedding—but I didn't know who *I* was. And I sure as hell didn't know what I represented.

This is why the Observation Car is important. You're not born knowing who you are. You're not going to know what you represent until you've lived a little. A kid doesn't know any of this stuff, and it's crazy to expect him to. But I felt tremendous pressure—knowing that my brothers were on track to becoming doctors and lawyers, each of them trying to outdo the others, all against a backdrop of state senators and federal judges and an endless number of attorney uncles—to pursue that life. That life was supposed to represent me, but it didn't. It never had.

But what was I going to do? Something different? It felt like insanity just contemplating the possibility. So one day, while I was still in high school, I wrote a suicide note. My grades were barely keeping me in school, while my friend Ross Perich was an excellent student and had already been accepted to UC Berkeley. I had no idea what I was going to do. I didn't fit in—not with my family, not with the path that was expected of me—and it gave me a perverse feeling of freedom to think of alternate possibilities. I could just check out. Just pull the plug. It wasn't a great plan, but it was an option.

I didn't go through with it—not then—but the fact that I even contemplated it shows the damage that can be done by pushing people to make decisions they're in no way capable of making. If I'd been given the time and the freedom to stand back and see the person I truly was, I would never have gone down that road. I like to think that I'd have figured out my love of art a lot sooner, that I'd have seen my own talent as valuable long before I tried to throw away my life. Questions like "Who are you?" and "What do you represent?" take a long time to answer—and they take even longer if you've already started telling yourself lies about the answers.

The reality is that we all tell ourselves lies. We're all story-tellers, and for most of us, these stories are fiction. It takes a lot of patience—and a lot of work to find that patience—to see ourselves clearly, to change the story and tell ourselves the truth.

But that work is all worthwhile. I have a friend who never found that patience. The lies he told himself started out innocuous enough, but when tragedy struck, they grew until they overcame every good thing he'd ever done with his life. His daughter was killed in a terrible drunk-driving accident. That in itself is enough to derail a man's faith in the world. But my friend had been sipping a nectar of lies for so long—"I've done my job as a father," "I deserve the peace of a predictable life,"

"The universe just wants to see me suffer"—that when the grief struck him, he made it all about himself. "You don't know my loss. You don't understand my pain." And because all he could see about himself was the pain he was experiencing, he fell out of recovery and abandoned his two surviving children. He let the story of his own pain's importance override all the other, healthier stories he could have told himself. Stories like, "I hurt, but I can grieve with my family" or "I hurt, but I won't heal without the people I love."

The lies that people tell themselves can be isolating and vicious. Further, like attracts like—and those lies pull in more negative energy. But if you set aside the impulse to tell yourself those lies, if you step away from the stories that only hurt you, you can replace them with stories that help you grow. You can be part of the solution to your own problems rather than perpetuating the challenges you face.

My friend Devon Jobes is a perfect illustration of this. When I first met Devon, he was nineteen years old, homeless, and deeply alcoholic. I mentored him for a few years, only to see him relapse time after time, until he stopped answering my calls.

Ten years later, he got serious about his sobriety and asked me to mentor him again. This time it stuck. He met a lovely woman named Fran. When they married, he asked me to be his best man. I was honored. Soon afterward, they had a beautiful baby girl, whom they named Charlotte. Together, they are incredibly loving people, happy, committed to their little family, and profoundly thankful for what they have. Their lives were so full of love that they decided to have a second child, another daughter, Lily.

Halfway through the pregnancy, they learned that Lily had a malformation of the heart: it was missing the right ventricle. The doctors were quite clear about what was going to happen: the moment Lily entered the world, she'd have to be rushed to open heart surgery. Some children with this condition can go on to live happy, healthy lives and some don't make it.

Devon and Fran weighed their options. They didn't want to terminate the pregnancy—Fran was Catholic, and Devon was a spiritual man in his own way—so they decided that they would do everything they could to ensure that Lily had the best possible chance at life.

They decided to have Lily at Ronald Reagan UCLA Medical Center, one of the best hospitals in the country. I visited dozens of times, sometimes bringing a whole posse of supportive well-wishers with me. Visiting was hard, especially seeing fragile little Lily hooked up to what looked like a dozen different machines. But the hardest part was seeing Devon and Fran. We'd all pray together. I prayed out loud and asked God to please let Lily live. But Devon corrected me. Instead, he said, "We're going to pray for God's will for Lily."

He knew that Lily didn't belong to him. He knew that Lily was a child of God, and that he didn't have the right to ask for anything so presumptuous as a life. He knew that complete surrender to God was the only way to get through this.

Months passed, and the day finally came when the doctors told Devon and Fran that there wasn't anything more they could do. They had to take Lily off life support, and they couldn't predict whether or not she'd survive.

She didn't.

I don't know how I would have reacted. I've never had a child of my own, but after those months of visiting that tiny baby in the NICU, I know that I loved her. And I know that Devon and Fran and little Charlotte loved her fiercely, and grieved her passing. I know that there is nothing in life harder than losing a child, but in all that grief, in all that pain, they never once turned away from each other. They walked together through this tragedy, and they walked with grace, and faith, and courage, and dignity. They taught me that you can't hold on, you can't grip life too tightly. Life is precious. And it isn't yours to begin with.

They kept their faith, and they made it through the hardest thing you can endure as a parent. A year and a half later, Devon and Fran got pregnant again. They kept going, and they had another little girl, Zoe—beautiful, healthy, and loving. The faith they kept, the story they lived their lives by, enabled them to live on. It let them find joy again.

I'm not saying that the particular faith that Devon and Fran clung to was necessarily the be-all and end-all of life. I was raised Catholic, and I still have my issues with the church. What I *am* saying is that Devon and Fran found a story that led them to health and happiness despite their terrible circumstances. It is important to recognize that some stories lead you to a healthier, more contented place, and others lead you into self-destructive circles.

When I first got sober, one of the most important conversations I had was with a man named Eric, who asked me how I envisioned my higher power. Eric hadn't grown up in a church, so he came to the conversation without any of the baggage I had, and I felt like I could be honest with him.

"Well," I said, dissolving a lump of sugar into my coffee, "distant, I guess. He was there once, but now he doesn't really come around—or care about me. He's not really in my life."

Eric shook his head as if he'd just heard a good joke, and said, "Now, tell me what your father was like when he was drinking."

It was like I'd been punched in the throat.

Eric went on to ask me what sort of God I'd have if I could design him from scratch.

"You can't actually create God," he said, "but if you could, what would he be like?"

I rattled off a list of attributes that characterized the exact opposite of the God I'd already described: "All powerful. Present. Loving. Caring. Forgiving. Just. Interested in me. Wants the best. A good sense of humor."

"Well, damn," Eric said. "That's a real higher power."

Eric and I talked a lot about God, and God's will. I'd always felt like I didn't know what God's will for me was, but I was pretty sure I knew what it wasn't. You know how you feel different when you're doing something that leads you in a good direction from when you're doing something that leads you in a bad one? You can feel it in your gut. Those feelings, those little whispers of moral intuition—it's all an influx of the Divine. It's God talking to you. If you're hopped up on booze and drugs, it's almost impossible to hear, but when you're clear, when you're sober, those little feelings ring true, like a bell. You have to listen—but they're there. You've probably felt them too.

I should draw a distinction between listening to *those* feelings and listening to the feelings that arise from the stories we tell ourselves. They can be tricky to separate. The other night I was driving home and ruminating on a series of terrible sinus headaches I'd had for several weeks, generally feeling miserable. And I caught myself telling one of those destructive stories: "I'm always sick. I'm never going to get better." You and I both know, in our rational minds, that no one is *always* sick (barring massive chronic conditions, of course). People with sinus headaches struggle but often eventually get better. That's the way a sinus headache works. It isn't permanent. But I wasn't feeling well, so I'd fallen into that old story. I kept it up late into the night too, only realizing what had happened at 4:00 a.m. when it suddenly hit me that I'd have to go about the rest of the day with this destructive attitude. And I decided that I wasn't going to be a victim of my own bullshit.

And that's really the trick—learning to tell the difference between your own BS and Divine influx. It requires careful listening. My old mentor Bob Palmer used to say that you could hear the Divine most clearly through meditation. I used to think that meant I'd have to go through years of meditation training to finally hear God's will for my life, but Bob was never a take-the-standard-route kind of guy.

I once went with Bob to dinner—he was supposed to be meeting a new mentee, a child actor who'd grown up and was trying to rebuild his career. This guy had already bounced around with a number of different (also very famous) spiritual teachers, and someone had finally directed him to Bob, almost as a last resort. So Bob and I brought this gent over to Fromin's Deli on in Santa Monica, and we ordered dinner. For the next forty-five minutes, we listened to this guy complain, almost without stopping for breath, about his career, his money, his marriage going to hell, his kids—everything. About forty minutes in, I'd had enough. I kept looking over at Bob like,

Come on, man; pull your Jedi mind trick stuff on this guy. We've got to cut him off.

That was when I realized that Bob had just taken that time to eat. Literally, Bob had spent the whole dinner nodding and grunting agreeably, and just eating. Just eating and listening. Not trying to steer this guy into some sort of epiphany. Not getting emotionally invested. He was taking care of himself and he was evaluating the whole situation.

Bob was a great listener. He listened to every word that guy said. I didn't know how to do that. But as soon as Bob had taken his last bite, he set his utensils down and wiped the corners of his mouth with his napkin. Bob was ready to talk.

He set down the napkin and said to the guy, "I hear you."

The guy didn't know that he was done talking, but he shut up anyway.

"Do you think," Bob started, "that you can go home tonight and sit down, and light a candle? Do you think you can do that?"

The guy looked uncertain—he'd just gushed about all his problems and now this great guru was asking him about candles?

"I can do that," he said.

"Do you think you can sit there and watch that candle for five minutes? Can you do that?"

"Yeah. I could do that."

"Then, after five minutes, just lean over and blow out the candle. Can you do that?"

"Yeah. I can do that."

"Good," Bob said. "We can start there." And he grabbed the check, and that was it.

Meditation can be a challenging concept. I am grateful my brother Danny and his wife, Tricia Ryan, introduced me to meditation. Most people don't know how to do it, I think. Or they consider it an advanced practice—something they'll tackle down the line, when they've gotten their other ducks in order. They're either intimidated by it or scared of it. But Bob knew that for some people, meditation was the bit that would really help, so that's where he began. Staring at a candle is the easiest place to start, and from there, you just add time, and eventually a mantra. Bob's mantra was deceptively simple:

> *I am here,*
> *as I am.*
> *So am I.*

Inhale on the first two lines, exhale on the last. *I am here, as I am* puts you in the now, and then lets you accept yourself. And then, that last line, *So am I,* invites God into the equation.

Eric had a great take on the concept of God. I had so many hang-ups on the topic that he once said to me, "I don't care what your God looks like; just get one." I had never heard anything like that. I believed that the strongest of men had faith, so I wanted to believe in something. In time, I came to realize that all the great religions have concepts similar to those I came up with that day. I realized we are all looking out different windows at the same sun.

When we're in the Observation Car, looking out at the world streaming past, we can sit still and see more clearly the stories we've always told. We can let go of our complaints—which inhibit our happiness—and refocus our energy, harnessing positivity. From here we can make healthier choices, listen to the voices of the Divine, and learn to distinguish between the will of a higher power and the stories—the lies—we tell ourselves.

CHAPTER 6

The Dining Car

UNLIKE THE OBSERVATION CAR, WHICH is built to
be a window to the surrounding landscape, the Dining
Car is its own little world. It's warmer than the other cars—all
wood paneling and thick curtains. Plush booths line either
side of the car, cradling tables set with white linen and a
single rose in a little bud vase. The aroma from the car's tiny
kitchen wafts over you, at once familiar and exotic, the smell of
childhood meals mingling with spices you can't quite identify.
Knives and forks clink against plates. There's the murmur of
conversation, sighs of contentment.

The tables around you neatly display different dishes.
There are demure, lightly dressed salads and big, juicy cheese-
burgers—the kind that require a fork and knife. Glossy
poached eggs on crisp greens and little goblets of Greek

yogurt topped with a smattering of berries and granola. Plates of creamy-sauced pastas and bowls filled with steaming curries. Fat wedges of cheesecake and perfect orbs of brightly colored sorbets.

You slide into an empty booth; pick up the expansive, leather-bound menu; and glance over its contents. The number of options seems staggering, especially coming from that tiny kitchen. Soon, someone will come by to take your order.

The Dining Car is all about sustenance. It's about satisfaction. It's about choice. The opportunity to take stock of our bodies and what they've been through. To figure out what they want—and what they need. This is where we go to get fed.

When I was born, back in 1963, hospitals didn't just allow smoking; they encouraged it. There was an ashtray at every patient's bedside. My mom lay in her bed, hours after I was born, with me in her arms and a cigarette between her lips. She smoked regularly from my first day on earth until I was thrown out of the house almost two decades later. All that second-hand smoke pumped into my lungs essentially made me a smoker too throughout my developmental years.

My body paid the price. I had constant bloody noses, unpredictable torrents of bright red that stained countless tissues, white T-shirts, and washcloths before fading to a deep rust color. The pain and pressure of chronic sinusitis built up behind my eyes, ached in my jaw, and never seemed to leave.

I eventually developed asthma too, the tightness wrapping around my chest and choking off my words. It felt like I was drowning in midair.

My health issues didn't stop there. During my senior year in high school, I lost about thirty-five pounds in thirty days. I looked emaciated, and I had chronic diarrhea and lots of bleeding. My mom took me to doctor after doctor. I sat in waiting rooms filled with people in their eighties and nineties—a seventeen-year-old kid wondering what the fuck was going on. There were so many tests. I suffered through barium enemas, in which they pumped thick, pink, chalky stuff up my ass until it felt like my insides were going to burst. I had upper and lower GI tests, and tubes and scopes were rammed into and out of my body.

But those tests produced no answers. I was essentially dying, fading away, and nobody knew why.

I could see the fear in my mother's eyes, the horror of watching her youngest being tormented by needles and probes and machines—and by his own body.

It wasn't just the smoke I had internalized; it was the stress of living in that house, of getting lost in the shuffle, left behind and ignored by my parents, and tormented by my stepsiblings. And as a result, I felt the pain of those years physically, to the point where I couldn't breathe. To the point where my insides were literally breaking down from the stress.

Someone once explained to me that when we undergo surgery, the anesthesia numbs our senses, but our bodies still feel the trauma—the slice of the scalpel, the tug and bruising of the retractors. We may be asleep, but our ears are still at work, capturing the whole thing: the incessant beeping of machines; the shrill, piercing sound of drill against bone; conversations about how broken we are. My body had absorbed it all, everything I'd been through, and it was telling my story, showcasing my pain in the only way it knew how, over and over again.

Finally, my mother got me to a top gastroenterologist who thought he might have a solution. There was a sulfa aspirin product, Sulfasalazine, that could maybe help. The doctor was very honest with me. "We don't really know how this works, he said, "but sometimes it does. We gave it to a lot of the GI cases coming back from the war, and it seemed to make a difference." Sulfasalazine, along with a bunch of steroids, brought me back from the brink. It saved my life. But the medicines could only do so much. Eventually, I'd have to listen to the story my body was telling, and work to change it, to heal.

I continued to take Sulfasalazine well into my thirties. At the time, I wasn't thinking about the side effects—I was just trying to stay alive. But the Sulfasalazine had rendered me impotent, something I wouldn't realize until much later when I was married and ready to start a family. After months of trying for a baby with no luck, doctors told me I probably wouldn't be able to have kids because of the prolonged exposure to the drug. The medicine that had saved my life had also ruined my sperm count. That news delivered a huge blow to my ego. I felt humiliated by the fact that my body couldn't accomplish what it had been built to do. The same "stories" I'd always told myself about my many failures crept back in. *I'm broken,* I told myself. *I'm defective. I'm contaminated.*

The shame of my shortcomings was exacerbated as the years went by, when friend after friend would share the good news of their pregnancies. They would introduce me to their beautiful children. It was incredible to see the features of my buddies reflected in the faces of their kids, to watch their mannerisms play out on a miniature scale. To see how fiercely they loved their kids, and the way those kids loved them back just as hard. To see how they taught them about the world. My friends were creating their own living legacies. I was thrilled for them, but with each new pregnancy, each birth, deep down I felt more acutely my own inability to procreate. I'd never have the chance to make the same impact.

Bob saw how much I was struggling, how hard it was for me to see these new lives and relationships evolve around me—relationships I thought I'd never have. One day, after the news came of yet another baby in my circle of friends, Bob pulled me aside.

"How many kids do you mentor?" he asked.

"About thirty-five," I responded.

He clapped a hand on my shoulder.

"You have children," he said with a smile, then walked away.

He was right. In that moment I realized that my brokenness was just another "story" I had been telling myself. *I'm always sick. I'm never going to get better. I'm defective. I'm contaminated.* None of those stories were true, and this one—that I would never be able to have children—wasn't true either. I still had the opportunity to pass on a part of myself to the next generation, and I was doing it. I had plenty of children, and they were flourishing.

Our bodies hold on to the trauma we've experienced, along with the "stories" we've told ourselves about them. Those "stories" can manifest as discomfort and pain, ailments and illnesses. But when we realize our agency—our ability to change the story about our bodies and their capacity, about our health and our worth—we can heal. We can learn to care for ourselves.

But first, we have to listen to what our bodies—and those "stories"—are trying to tell us.

Not long after my divorce, I went in for a regular physical with my internist. As I sat on the exam table, the paper bunching under my thighs, he ran through the usual checklist of questions about my health.

"How are you feeling?" he asked.

I told him about the end of my marriage. About the grief I'd been experiencing.

"I'm just really bummed out," I said. "Really, really sad."

"Do you want me to prescribe you some antidepressants?" he asked, jotting something down on my chart.

I looked at him, felt my brow furrow. *This is odd,* I thought. *There were no tests done.* "What would you prescribe?" I asked.

"Prozac," he said. "I can write you a script right now."

Before I could respond, he pulled a pen from his pocket, grabbed his prescription pad and scribbled a few lines. He tore off the sheet and handed it to me.

"Here," he said. "This should help."

I was baffled by how easily that prescription had landed in my hand. I held in my palm the potential to numb myself to it all, one pill at a time. But I was done with that. I never filled the prescription. It hurt like hell, but I was going to feel it all. It was grief. Part of the human process.

A friend chose the numbing route. He had been prescribed antidepressants during his divorce, and he took them all the way through. When he came out on the other side, he told me how grateful he was for those little pills.

"You know," he said, "I never would have gotten through my divorce without those antidepressants."

How would he ever know? Maybe he was right. Maybe he couldn't have made it through. But taking those pills also meant he didn't have to address his vulnerabilities—the reckless spending and gambling and womanizing that were compounding the hurt he could no longer feel.

The antidepressants prevented him from going through the excruciating pain that could've helped him address his shortcomings. Maybe he couldn't have gotten through it without pharmaceutical assistance . . . but maybe he could have. And maybe he would've wound up better off. Stronger. I saw him continue his irresponsible spending habits and womanizing well after his divorce, and I have seen it cost him two relationships since.

Your body knows wrong from right. Symptoms like discomfort, pain, and depression are a call from the universe, letting you know that it's time to reevaluate—that it may be time to make some changes. I call it Divine influx; the universe is trying to talk to you.

I've learned that the natural emotion of depression is as important as joy. Sometimes you have to hit some sort of bottom—a place where you can't deny the fact that things aren't working, or that you're painfully, devastatingly unhappy—before you can find a way back up. As William Blake wrote,

"You never know what is enough unless you know what is more than enough."

Of course, clinical depression and chemical imbalances are a different story. There's certainly a time and place for medication. But I've worked with plenty of people—especially adolescents—who have been offered prescriptions like Skittles. Instead of encouraging them to listen to those feelings, we facilitate their erasure. That frightens me. Our feelings are the messengers of our intuition. The uncomfortable ones are trying to tell us something, and it's up to us to listen. It's the only way to grow.

You have to know the story you've been telling in order to change it.

At my first wedding, we picked a wedding song by Barry White: "Can't Get Enough of Your Love, Babe." It wasn't exactly original, but it was a true classic, one that certainly felt right when we chose it. There was a downside to picking a classic like that though: it's a cultural mainstay. After my divorce, I heard it all the time. On the radio, in random Starbucks and grocery stores, at parties. Barry seemed to taunt me in his smooth baritone:

Baby, it didn't take all of my life to find you,
But you can believe it's gonna take the rest of my life to keep you.

It hadn't worked out that way. I hadn't been able to keep her. I had always loved the song, but hearing it became depressing.

It was a reminder that I had failed at marriage, that I'd probably spend the rest of my life alone. Whenever it came on, I had to turn off the radio, leave the coffee shop, or go somewhere else.

Many years later, I flew up to Sacramento, California, to see my goddaughter and niece, Ashley, get married. I watched from my seat as she and her new husband shared a slow, sweet first dance to their own wedding song. I was thrilled for her. The love in the room was palpable, and I was so glad to be a part of it. But when that song ended, the first strains of "Can't Get Enough of Your Love, Babe" came blaring through the speakers. I cringed. I wanted to take a walk, find somewhere out of earshot, just for a couple of minutes.

But before I could get up, Ashley came over, grabbed my hands, and dragged me onto the dance floor. Every fiber in my being wanted to make a run for it, but I couldn't turn down the beautiful bride. I started to dance with her, somewhat half-heartedly at first. All those feelings of failure were still lodged in my consciousness, and I felt them weighing me down. But seeing how joyful Ashley was, hearing the percussive beat that rolls through the song, the swell of horns as the chorus approached, I couldn't help but feel my own heart swell. We were grooving. All I felt was happiness. And I finally let go of the "story" I had been telling about my own marriage.

Ashley didn't realize it at the time, but she was creating a whole new story around that song for me. That moment made me recognize that everything I had been through—the divorce included—was all a part of a journey, one that had made me a better me, brought me to a better place. I wasn't a failure; I was resilient, capable of giving and receiving love in important and meaningful ways. There was so much of it in this room, in my life in general. There was so much more to come. Now, I was ready for it.

When it came to my health, I had to change my "story" too. I had to change the things I was focused on. I had to change the statements that were coming out of my mouth—that I was broken, sick, defective, and more. I had to stop using the word *chronic*. I had to stop saying *my* asthma, *my* colitis. I had to tap into the power of the spoken word.

Clay, my mentor told me, "James, you have so much energy. The good news is when you're on the upswing, you're totally stoked. Your enthusiasm is palpable; it's contagious. But unfortunately the reverse is also true. That same abundance of energy can pull you in the opposite direction."

He was right. Enthusiasm comes from the Greek word *enthousiasmos*, which translates to "inspiration or possession by a god." It's incredibly powerful. Without it, it's easy to find yourself plummeting to new lows. No matter where I'm headed, I tend to pick up steam quickly. That's true for most of us, and it's why it's so crucial to pay attention to where you're heading—positive or negative. I started to focus on positivity, on being healthy, eating well, exercising, and taking care of myself. And it made all the difference.

I never got to meet Elisabeth's father, Julian Weinstock, but I've heard countless stories about him. Julian was Jewish. He was just a boy when his family heard that the Nazis were coming to occupy Poland, where they lived. So, they sent him away, hoping for his survival. He escaped, but the rest of his family wasn't so lucky. All of them—his mother, father, brothers, and sisters—were killed. They were among the millions of Jews murdered by Hitler and his followers.

Julian went on to build his own family and successful life in the US. But that trauma stayed with him. It meant Elisabeth didn't get much of him while he was alive. Hitler was not only responsible for the murder of millions of Jews; his actions and toxic rhetoric continue to leave its mark. And Hitler used the power of the spoken word to do it. People don't always grasp its potential. The spoken word can lift people up, help them heal, and change their lives, but it has also fueled some of history's greatest atrocities. That's how incredible its impact is.

Imagine if, instead, we could focus our energy into the positive, pointing the power of the spoken word in the direction of truth, love, helping, acceptance, forgiveness. What could we accomplish? How could you transform your own story, or the ones of those you love and countless others whom you've never met?

Each morning, one of the first things I do is repeat an affirmation: "I am grateful and I love my life. I am grateful and I love my life. I am grateful and I love my life." I say it out loud—as loudly as I can. It can start out feeling a little ridiculous, then funny. That's when I realize just how true it is. It forces me to look around at my surroundings, to think about the day in front of me—one where I get to kiss my beautiful partner, Elisabeth, and hug my incredible dog, Duke, and head off to do the work I love. I am one of the few lucky people in this world who gets to say, "I love what I do and I love everyone I do it with." It changes the story. I can actually feel the energy shift, that prophecy fulfilling itself. If I say so.

Next, no matter the day, no matter how I'm feeling, I write a gratitude list. I write down ten things I'm grateful for every single day. It's one of the most powerful tools that I've employed, the key to the Law of Attraction—the route to abundance, wealth, love, joy, true happiness, and success. Your subconscious cannot distinguish between reality and what you tell it. It believes whatever you say. When you send your subconscious the message that you're grateful, it believes you, and the universe rewards you with more to be grateful for. Your perspective changes, and you act accordingly.

Elisabeth embodies that truth. I am so blessed to have her in my life. She shows me unconditional love, and accepts me for who I am. We have so much in common: we love helping others; we love the water, surfing, skateboarding, and punk rock. Our values and beliefs align. And she demonstrates the power of pursuing a clean, spiritual path. Every morning, she journals extensively—sometimes for half an hour, sometimes forty-five minutes. She writes letters to God, expressing her gratitude. And she pays it forward.

Almost everything she does throughout the day is designed to help someone else. Elisabeth has worked with an East Side Latino gang for more than twenty years, mentoring countless men and women, boys and girls, helping them through adversity and the challenges of the streets. She created a class in the community center nearby—aptly titled "Life"—to teach basic life skills: how to shake hands with people and look them in the eye, how to open a checking account, how to do the basic things that so many of us take for granted.

While some of the people with whom she has worked have continued their ways, winding up in prison or worse, a lot of others have ended up on the straight and narrow. They've found a way out, a path forward, and she continues to work with them today. She has an enormous heart. Everything she does is a real inspiration to me. And she is in my life today because I got grateful and real about my potential to be loved.

I had seen it modeled before. My paternal grandparents were so sweet with one another. They had this adorable, playful romance. We would go to brunch with them on Sundays to The Spinnaker in Sausalito, and my grandpa would always head toward my grandma, saying, "Let me go sit next to my girlfriend." They had been together for decades, and they still had so much love between them. Through them, I saw that love was real and attainable. I chose to believe it. And because I was willing to be open long enough, I met Elisabeth. She showed me that it's never too late, that I was right to never give up on love.

I can pull up so many other examples from my life about how changing my perspective and choosing gratitude changed my life, and all that the universe brought into it, but there's one particular story that stands out.

I had developed a multimillion-dollar production company on Wilshire Boulevard in Beverly Hills—a lifelong dream. I thought I had done it, peaked. I had everything I'd ever wanted. But one day, that dream would collide with another one, and I'd realize how much further I could go.

On that fateful day, I skateboarded to the café up the street from my office for a coffee and joined the line out front. Standing in front of me was this guy in a white T-shirt and jeans, blue Vans on his feet. He had a mop of curly blond hair. I caught his profile out of the corner of my eye. *Oh my God,* I thought to myself, *is that Stacy Peralta?* It was.

Stacy had been a professional skateboarder and surfer, and he was my idol growing up. I had his poster right over my bed when I was twelve. I had spent hours cutting pictures of him out of *Skateboarder* magazine as a kid. And not only was he a killer skateboarder—one of the best in the world—but he went on to become an incredible filmmaker too. I had always wanted to meet him, and there he was, chatting with his wife, right in front of me.

Normally, I wouldn't want to bother someone; in L.A. you see famous people all the time, and I know how hard it can be to get a little privacy. But I had a connection to this guy—he had inspired me in so many ways. I had to say something.

"Excuse me, Stacy Peralta?" I said.

He turned around.

"Yeah?"

"My name is James Sweigert and I'm a huge fan. I had your poster over my bed when I was twelve. Sorry to interrupt; I just had to say something."

His face broke into a huge smile, and he looked down to see my skateboard. It was an N-Men board. The N-Men are a crew of hardcore skateboarders from Sacramento. They started skating together in 1975 and never stopped. They were pretty underground—skating empty pools throughout Northern California—but they had influenced some of the sport's greats, and I had grown up with them. We'd drifted apart, and then when we reconnected years later, they sent me the board. I explained to Stacy that they had been my crew.

"Get out of here!" he said. "What are you up to now?"

"I have a film and television production company right here," I told him. "We design main titles too. What are you working on?" I asked him.

"I'm working on a documentary about Eddie Aikau," he said.

I had become less of a skater over the years and more of a surfer, but I knew who Eddie Aikau was. He was a legendary big-wave surfer from the North Shore of Oahu in Hawaii. And he was also a true hero. Eddie was the first lifeguard at Waimea Bay, a particularly treacherous body of water. He had risked his life to save more than five hundred people who almost drowned in its waters. Not a single person died on his watch. He would go out trying to save others too.

In 1978, he was serving as a crewmember on Hokule'a, a voyaging canoe making the journey between Hawaii and the Tahitian islands, when the boat capsized. He tried to paddle out on his surfboard to get help, but never made it. While the other members of the crew were eventually rescued, he was never found; he just vanished into the deep, blue Hawaiian seas, never to be seen again.

I knew the story. I had done a lot of surfing on the North Shore. I'd been dragged across the reef at Pipeline too. And I knew just how amazing Eddie had been. I think I may have actually dropped to my knees and grabbed Stacy's shirt.

"Please, Stacy," I said, half joking, "please let me design the main titles for this film."

He laughed.

"Let me talk to the director and the other producers. It's good timing though, because we're just starting to look at this stuff."

"I'd love to do it, man," I said, this time from my feet.

Then, I did what any superfan would do: I had him autograph my skateboard.

Back at the office, I immediately started researching the project's director, Sam George, and the other producers and calling them.

"Hey," I said, "I just ran into Stacy Peralta and heard about your film. I understand the gravity of this story—how important and sensitive it is. I'd love to contribute."

They gave me a shot, agreeing to let me design the main titles.

The film's director, Sam George, came to the office to take a look at the titles we had put together. They were beautiful, in this font that was at once historical and yet contemporary. The letters popped against a black surface, the blue of the tide rippling through them before the words slowly drifted away, mirroring the story itself.

"That's it," Sam said. He didn't have any changes or notes—something that never happens in this business.

The whole experience was remarkable, but that wasn't the end of it—not even close. Not only did I get to create and produce the main titles for a film about a man I so admired, and not only did the project pay (though I would have gladly done it for free), I also got to attend the premiere in Oahu with my business partner and creative director, Nate Howe.

There, I met Eddie Aikau's family—his brothers, Sol and Clyde, and his sister, Myra. They invited me to the very sacred opening-day ceremony of the Eddie Aikau Big Wave Invitational, a surf competition held in his memory. I was so excited that I couldn't sleep the night before.

In the morning, the surfers stood in a circle with their boards behind them, listening to the words of a Hawaiian priest, before doing a ceremonial paddle-out for Eddie. I felt like I was three feet off the ground the whole time, levitating on the magic of the experience. That film we worked on together went on to win an Emmy.

Stacy Peralta's impact on my life—facilitated by the will of the universe—didn't end there either. At that coffee shop, I had been telling him all about my experience with the N-Men, not only to explain where I had come from, but also because I thought their story could be the basis for his next documentary.

But he looked at me and said, "James, you were sitting on the edge of the half-pipe in these pools watching these guys. You've got great perspective. Why don't *you* tell the story?"

With his encouragement, I decided to take the project on, to create a documentary that I've been writing, producing, and directing for nine years—and that is now in the final stages of postproduction. Everything has come full circle. I made room in my life for the universe to come through, and it did.

The only thing more powerful than finding gratitude every day is having people to share it with. So I share my list with the group I mentor, and they do the same. I'm constantly drafting and receiving lists. The day Devon's daughter Lily died, he sent me his list of ten things he was grateful for that day, which was very likely the worst day of his life. That hit me like a ton of bricks, the fact that he was still able to find things to be grateful for in the presence of so much pain. But it was his story to tell: if he said there were things to be grateful for, even on that impossibly difficult day, there were. He could find a reason to keep moving.

I shared this lesson with my friend Charlie Aguero. By all accounts, Charlie has an enviable life. He has a wonderful wife and children and a great career working as creative director for the NFL. One day he gave me a call.

"Hey, James," he said.

I could hear in his voice that something was off. He sounded down, depressed.

"What's up?" I asked.

Charlie told me that he had just been diagnosed with multiple sclerosis. He was devastated.

"I don't know what to do, man," he said. "It's going to be so hard."

If you say so, I thought.

Then I had an idea. One of my protégés, Jack Osbourne, had been diagnosed with multiple sclerosis about four years earlier. He was married, with three children of his own and a very successful career as a producer and director. He was living with MS, and he was thriving. Jack had also started doing a lot of advocacy work, even launching a media campaign to share his experience with the disease, to show that it wasn't the death sentence so many people imagine.

"If you say it will be hard, Charlie, it will be," I told him. "Where are you? I'm going to come get you right now."

I called Jack from my car.

"Hey," I said. "One of my guys has just been diagnosed with MS. I know you've been living with it. Can we come by? Can you tell him what it's been like for you?"

"Of course. Come on over," Jack said.

I picked up Charlie and drove over to Jack's house. Jack introduced Charlie to his three daughters before bringing us into the kitchen. We sat around the table as Jack told his story. A few things had changed since his diagnosis: he was now more focused on eating well and exercising, on pacing himself, and he now took his medication regularly (and still does today). But overall, Jack was then, and is now, living a full, robust life. We still surf together, and he still takes his little girls on hikes. He camps, climbs, and does all the other things that make him happy. And he doesn't take any of it for granted.

I have been saying for thirty years that the two most powerful words in our language are "me too." When you remove the ability for someone to say, "You couldn't possibly understand," it eliminates any defense. Sympathy is good but there is nothing more powerful than empathy. This is why survivor groups are helpful: it is important to find people who struggle with what you struggle with, who are going through what you are going through. Helping others, sharing our experience and victories is a true service to humankind, and it is essential to our growth and healing.

One such teacher is one of my favorites, Fr. Tom Weston. He talks about how everyone has his or her own personal hell. He says, "There is no such thing as normal people, just people who haven't shared honestly with you yet." Compassion is everything.

Suddenly the story changed for Charlie. He had new information—the truth—of what it could be like to live with MS. He could treat it, and maintain all the parts of his life that brought him joy—including, most importantly, his career and his family. Today, he's living in acceptance.

Not too long ago, I stopped by Charlie's office at the NFL just to pay him a visit.

"Come in," he said. "Have a seat."

I sat across from him and scanned the room. There were pictures of his family, framed sketches he'd done, and a shelf of awards, complete with six Emmys. He also had a big white-board stretching across one wall. At the top of the board, he had written, "If you say it's going to be hard, it will be." He had credited me with the quotation.

Wow, I thought. Charlie had found my words important enough to hang in his office. I was amazed that they'd had such an impact on him, that they'd helped him change the story about his disease. My mother used to say, "Watch your mouth!" She was right. The words that come out of our mouths have an impact. What we say sets the tone not just for our days, but also for our lives. That's the power of the spoken word. And that quotation written—*manifested*—up on Charlie's board inspired me to tell my story in order to help you tell yours. And to change it, if need be.

As my brother Paul said, "You're in control, man." You have to be the conductor, and your words and actions set the tone. If we choose to dwell on negativity, steer our ship toward the dark stormy clouds, then things break down, we can't press on, and we find ourselves in rough seas. But if we focus on what's good, on what's working, and point our ship toward that beautiful golden sunset, it's going to be smooth sailing.

It's also up to you to care for that train, to ensure that it's in working order and on the right track. You have to do the things that make you feel good. Some of this stuff is pretty basic, and we learn it in kindergarten: diet and exercise. Our teachers cover the basic food groups, the importance of eating a well-balanced diet. They teach you in recess to run around and play, to get a move on! You learn the value of feeling good.

Part of my self-care is surfing: the sun on my shoulders, the salt water splashing in my face. The way it feels to practice patience, the most important element of the sport, according to Kelly Slater. Waiting for the right wave, popping up on my board when the time comes, and riding it all the way to the beach. The experience is invigorating.

Making love to the woman I adore. Living cleanly. Eating well. Gratitude. Meditation. Service. All of it helps me to feel good, reassert my worth, and realize my own agency in life.

Taking care of yourself helps to change the story, to show your mind and your body that maybe there's another truth out there for you. If you've been telling yourself the same kinds of "stories" I did—that you're defective, broken, a disappointment, that there's nowhere for you to go—then taking the time to care for yourself—to practice gratitude, to flip the script—can help. But you have to buy into that truth.

One of my old mentors, Milton Dicus, had the greatest line: "The only handicap in life is a bad attitude." Pretty poignant, especially coming from a guy who was plagued with more than his fair share of handicaps, including a severe case of advanced Parkinson's disease. Pain is mandatory in life, but misery's optional. Why not ensure that your train is in working order, so that you can follow those tracks right on toward the beautiful sunset? Why not believe? What if our best days are actually ahead of us? Why not hope? Why not focus on that? When we listen to our bodies and hear what they're trying to tell us, we can make the choice to change our stories, to thrive. I believe God wants us to flourish, to be amazing, and thus help crack others open to do the same!

CHAPTER 7

The Bar Car

THE BAR CAR IS LOUD and bustling. The place is already loose and booze-soaked, as if the party's been going on for hours; you can smell it when you walk through the door. An older gentleman bangs out jazz tunes on a piano, throwing his whole body into it. The music and conversation are punctuated by the occasional cackle or whoop from the crowd. Bodies are crammed around the bar, a broad mahogany slab that feels too large for the space. The lighting is soft and low, and everyone kind of glows, looking as if they've been lit from within.

Outside, it's dark. With the way the light bounces around the car, the train seems to be passing through a void. The only indication that you're moving is the slight sway under your feet, and the occasional lurching of the people around you. You approach the bar and run your palms over its lacquered edge. A woman in a pink turtleneck and pearls sits to your right, her back ramrod straight, sipping on what has to be a club soda and glaring at the scene unfolding around her. There's a couple to your left, both of them propped up on their elbows, their faces threatening to fall into one another, legs entangled. A ruddy-cheeked, bearded man is slumped in one of the chairs in the corner, emitting loud, open-mouthed snores. His lips curl into a smile with each exhale.

The Bar Car is where you come to forget it all: your responsibilities, vulnerabilities, pain, awkwardness, and inhibitions. With your escape of choice in hand, the warmth spreading into your limbs, the night is rife with possibility. Your body and your brain feel more at ease. The rest of the world—the stress of work, difficult relationships, the disapproving stare of the woman beside you—fades almost to black.

You strike up a conversation with the bartender. Her eyes are locked on yours. You're making jokes, telling stories. She's from a town near yours, knows some of the same people. You're bonding over your common history. The couple to your left is falling in love before your eyes; you're sure of it.

You finish a story you're sure is hilarious, and the bartender laughs appreciatively. But as she turns to help another customer, you see her roll her eyes in your direction. You look back to your left. The couple is arguing now. One of them throws a wad of cash on the bar and storms out. The glow of the car seems to dim. The ring stains on the bar become more apparent, along with the tracks in the carpet and the stale-beer-and-cigarettes smell that has sunk into your clothes. Outside, the world continues to rush past, but you can't see a thing.

Growing up, alcohol and drugs were an institution in my house. There was drinking every night. Someone was always drunk or high, my parents included. It was the norm, just part of the everyday workings of our dysfunctional family. And though booze made my mom more unpredictable—and more likely to take her frustration out on me—when I tried it for myself at twelve, I also saw the other side of it. Liquor smoothed the edges of my existence, made everything feel lighter.

I didn't drink every day, but when I did, I drank until the lights went out. In Sacramento, where you could ride a horse over the levee through the cottonwoods along the American River all the way up to the foothills of the Sierra Nevada, we called it "cowboy drinking." The Irish call it "time travel" . . . and indeed, I was transported: I'd wake up in Reno. I'd wake up in fields. I once headed from Sacramento to Eugene, Oregon, for a graduation. I came to the next day in Walla Walla, Washington. I'd missed the graduation and driven one state too far. I'd wake up inside rolled cars and next to busted-up motorcycles without a clue how any of it had happened. And I just kept going.

Pot and cocaine followed, along with the occasional mushrooms and acid. The harder my life felt, the more I did. It was a cycle I couldn't escape. Drinking and drugs were the only things that distracted me from everything I knew was wrong with me, all the ways I didn't measure up, all the trauma I had endured. My family had abandoned me, and alcohol and drugs allowed me to abandon the world, to forget all about reality, to time travel into nothingness. It didn't matter where I woke up; there was no one next to me when I did.

Even when I was homeless, when I had nothing but a skate-board with which to get around and nothing but the redwoods for shelter, I spent what money I could scrape together on booze. Hiding bottles around town meant I wouldn't have to go too long without a drink. Addiction became my whole story.

I looked the part too. My hair was scraggly, and I had a raggedy beard to match. An old girlfriend's dad had been a pilot in Vietnam, and years earlier she had given me his flight suit. That's what I wore as I rode my skateboard around, bottle to bottle, barely coherent. My look made me a fixture downtown, along with the hookers, who called me Jet Man.

"Hey, Jet Man," they'd yell as I skated by.

"Good evening, ladies," I'd reply, on my way to the next bottle.

I told myself that drugs and alcohol were my only real friends, and they stuck with me while I slept under trees and on other people's couches and in flimsy makeshift beds in shitty downtown flats. They were there until that final suicide attempt, when all the stories I had been telling myself came to a head. I was a disappointment, a failure, and most of all, I was completely alone in the world. Useless and unlovable, and thus invisible—and rightfully so.

That night I sat there alone, getting drunk enough to black out. I was alone when I climbed into my truck. Alone when I drove my car directly into that tree, with no one to hear the screech of my tires, the sound of metal crunching as it slammed into bark, the engine screaming from the impact, finally relenting as I put the truck in reverse and swerved back onto the road. I was alone when I determined that my not dying from the crash had been a mistake, and that I would have to right the wrong of my survival.

Back at my apartment, the key slid into place with a hollow *thunk*, a quiet nod affirming my decision to off myself. There was no one to hear me weep over my last-ditch attempt, when I failed to find bullets or rope and finally headed to the bathroom, the sound of my howling echoing off the walls, off the tub that refused to fill.

But when my brother David arrived, sitting with me in the wee hours of the morning while I ranted about every wrong that that had ever been done to me, when he heard me ask for help and listened, when he sat next to me in the back row of that first meeting, I had to admit that I wasn't alone—not anymore, at least. For the first time, I had to reevaluate my story. I had to question its truth.

I hadn't always been alone. I had gotten a lot of love, and not just from years one to seven, when my mom was still present and attentive. I remembered visiting my Aunt Sally and Uncle Jack's Whiffletree Ranch in Carmel Valley. Aunt Sally had been so kind to me, treating me the way my mom had when I was little, when it was just her and me. Uncle Jack was a horse whisperer before that was even a term. He taught me how to rope and ride like a real cowboy. He was also a very successful western artist. Actors James Cagney, Ronald Reagan, Tom Selleck, and Sam Elliott all collected his work. In his sacred studio on the ranch he taught me how to paint, how to lay a base coat down, and the importance of that. He showed me how to take in the landscape and capture on Masonite board the way the light filtered through the clouds.

And even after my oldest brother, Billy, left home for college, he still came back to see me. My brothers would pluck me from the chaos for weekend camping trips. I wasn't alone when we drove out to the middle of nowhere, until the pavement turned to dirt. We pitched our tents as the sun went down and huddled together as it got dark, a fire blazing in front of us and a vast expanse of stars blinking over our heads. They loved me. They'd remembered me. They'd cared enough to come back.

My dad's wife—my stepmother, Trudi—cared too. She'd had two daughters of her own, but never a little boy, and when I came to visit she gave me love and support, and always asked me questions about my life and my interests.

The "story" I had been telling about my mom and stepdad wasn't what I had always imagined it to be either.

I finally allowed myself to see it all—how my stepfather and stepsiblings were coming to live with us in those early years after their own mother's passing only a year earlier, how much my mom had been through, the progress she'd made. I recognized that the thing I resented her for the most, the fact that she worked so hard to help everyone she could, was the best trait I got from her.

That same impulse lives within me too, powered in part by my biology. Following a five-and-a-half-hour heart surgery, I found out I was born with a fifth artery coming right out of the top of my heart. I literally have more heart than the average guy—and more love too. It's why working with people to tap into their immense potential fuels my engine.

And thanks to my mom, I learned something that comes to her naturally: that helping others is a wonderful mission—as long as it doesn't mean you lose track of the people you love. I now know my mother and stepfather did the very best they could, and I know they worked very hard to keep us fed and to keep a roof over our heads.

Over the years, she and my stepfather, Cass, saved each other. They had to go through their own growing pains, sure, but they eventually became the selfless and loving people the universe intended them to be. I love them both deeply. Not only have they modeled for me a successful long-term relationship, today my mom and Cass show up for everyone, attending every grandkid's recital, graduation, and wedding. They spend most mornings at church, and most afternoons driving elderly relatives to doctors' appointments. Every single day they show how much they care. They are incredible.

Mom eventually made her way back to me too, and I forgave her. I accepted her, and I found a love for her as true and deep as any relationship could be. Despite our rocky years, she had a real impact on me, and I'm proud to say I think I had a similar impact on her. To this day, I keep a letter that she wrote to me more than twenty years ago. It was the January after I had moved to Los Angeles. We had just thrown her a birthday party, trying to capture what she meant to the people lucky enough to know her.

Dearest Jimmy,

I just can't thank you enough for the wonderful birthday. The party was perfect. I loved the picture with all the writings on it, and your video is too much. But the greatest gift you probably aren't aware of—to the mother who just muddled along, trying to do her

*best, feeling insignificant in the scheme of things—you
gave a feeling of worth, a sense of success, and some
credibility. I can't thank God enough for you and all
the blessing he has given me and I pray he will bless
you in this new year.*

Thank you, Jimmy.

I love you.

—Mother

It was the first time she'd told me how proud of me she was,
how much I had made a difference in her life. Every day, I hope
she knows how much of a difference she has made in mine.

My mother just had her ninetieth birthday. I'm very grateful
that she is still around, but I know someday she won't be.
When she passes, I'm sure that all of Sacramento will come
to the funeral, and we'll all have to grapple with the loss of a
truly incredible woman. But like all the people I've lost over
the course of this beautiful, brutal thing called life, I know
she'll still be with me, alive and well in my heart, cheering for
the person I've become.

But in the Bar Car, there's no need for revelations like these.
The music and the booze fill the silence so you don't have to
think about where you've been or where you're headed—or
about what's true and what's not.

The term *Bar Car* is not necessarily to be interpreted literally in terms of escapes like alcohol, drugs, and nicotine, although it can be. It's anything in life—food, phones, social media, toxic relationships—that blocks our intuition, that Divine influx that Eric had so clearly laid out in the conversations we had about God. It's the stuff that clouds our judgment, that prevents us from feeling when something isn't quite right. Instead, it lets us off the hook. That's what the Bar Car is all about. There, your story is what you make it; you don't have to analyze it.

I had been badly hurt; there was no doubt about that. But I had also pushed a lot of people away with my anger. My acerbic tongue had acted as a barrier, making it hard for anyone to get close to me. Even my humor had served as a moat. I'd been committed to ensuring my own loneliness.

A long while back, I called one of my dear friends, Kurt, for advice. He told me to sit down, and grab a pen and paper. He said, "Write this sentence: DO . . ." He had me write each word, one at a time, and right after he delivered the last one, he hung up on me. I looked down, still cradling the phone between my shoulder and ear. On a legal pad I had scrawled, "DO NOT BELIEVE EVERYTHING YOU THINK." I just sat there staring at it. It was brilliant. My own mind had been leading me astray, and I had been following it blindly. If I could question my rationale, I could change my story. I could find the solution.

But in the Bar Car, there's no need to be accountable. That's why it's so easy to get stuck there. One drink turns into two, then five. The hours begin to unspool, one after another. Suddenly, you've forgotten about your engine entirely. You're not thinking about the coal that needs shoveling to keep things moving, or that you're nearing a way station and it might be a good time to unload some baggage. And even when the shine of the car starts to wear off and it stops feeling good in there, you still can't leave. You're not sure where to go, or what you're heading back to. You're not sure how to find the truth.

But if you can slide off that stool and get yourself to the other side of the door, even just for a little bit, you can see the Bar Car for what it is: a set of distractions that clouds your decision making, blurring the lines between wrong and right. The first piece of the puzzle is knowing what those distractions are. When you do, you can address them. It doesn't mean you have to leave forever; for many of us it's fine to visit from time to time. But if you're spending all your time there, that train's going to run out of steam, and you'll be dead on your tracks. That's unfortunate, because there's so much more to see.

When you're not in the Bar Car, your channels are clear. You can feel when something's wrong, and you can feel when it's right. That's God talking to you, and when you can listen, you can let that intuition guide you. As you make your way along your path toward the things you truly want—that pie-in-the-sky job, that beautiful house, that fulfilling relationship, or whatever it may be—the universe will move shit around to make way for you. But, as my old business partner, Nate, would say, you have to be able to listen to the whispers, to tune in and change direction if need be.

In the Bar Car, I couldn't really hear anything; no one can. While it seemed to protect me from my truth, it also prevented me from escaping it. I could blot out the world with booze, pot, and coke until I was blind to it, but when my vision returned, I was always still me, and I felt just as useless as I had before my first sip.

It's important to note that we all end up in the Bar Car for a reason. For me, the drinking, the drugs, and even the sarcasm were all survival techniques that I had employed as a kid. Sure, they were unhealthy, but they had served me, helped me survive the tumult and dysfunction of my home life; they had their place. In their own way, they had kept me alive through some of my darkest times. But if I ever wanted to change my story, to really listen, I'd have to leave those techniques behind. I'd have to step away from the Bar Car and find other ways to cope.

From the outside looking in, I could see the Bar Car for what it really was. And when I took the first step to leave it behind, I was able to see not only my truth—the vulnerabilities that led me to drinking and drugs—but also my potential. I'd have to start, though, by figuring out what I had to work with.

At first, I felt lower than a snake turd in a wagon track. I had no idea who the fuck I was, but I was sure it was someone awful. My first mentor knew that this was the first story that had to change, so he sat me down, handed me a pen, and slid a fresh sheet of binder paper across the table.

He said, "When a man takes inventory of his store, he doesn't only take inventory of what's been sold and what's been shoplifted. He takes inventory of what's still on the shelves. I want you to write down all of your positive attributes."

It seemed reasonable enough. I wanted to do this, to get better. I had nothing left to lose, after all. But as I gripped the pen, the tip poised over the paper, nothing came. I looked at him and shook my head.

"I don't—"

"Think about it," he encouraged.

It took a while, but I eventually came up with three positive things to say about myself. I was stuck after that, but it was a start.

He folded the paper in half and handed it to me.

"There's a lot you're gonna need to get rid of, but a lot of good that you're gonna keep," he said. "This is part of the good stuff. Put it in a file folder. Pull it out when you have a moment of self-doubt."

My mentor and the friends I'd met through meetings would encourage me to see the worth in my engine, and how it could come to life with a little coaxing. One woman I'd met, named Wendy, sat across from me at a Denny's, feeding back to me the qualities she had seen in me.

"Write this down," she said, pulling a pen from her purse and tapping it against the paper place mat in front of me. "You're creative," she said. "You're funny." I dutifully wrote down everything she said until I had a long list in front of me. I stared at it.

That's who I am? I thought. *Someone sees all that in me?* It was a beautiful experience, and it helped me to believe in my own value. I still have that place mat.

Over time, I grew to see those things in myself, and to believe that they were true. Since then, I've added many more attributes to the list. I realized the things I cared about mattered too, that I could pursue art, comedy, creativity—all the things that lit me up. They had a place in the world, just like medicine or law or politics, and they could fuel my train in the direction of that beautiful sunset.

Listing those positive attributes is a powerful tool. I tell all my mentees to do the same thing, to list as many positive things about themselves as they can. But there's a catch.

"You're going to get stuck," I tell them, "And that's when you have to get some feedback. You're gonna need to go to your friends, your family, your wife, or husband and ask them to tell you what your positive attributes are."

We all get caught up in the minutiae of our lives. It's easy to forget the real value we bring to the table. And sometimes our loved ones are more focused on telling us we forgot to screw the cap back on the toothpaste than on sharing the amazing qualities they see in us, or letting us know how special we are. But we all need to hear it—from ourselves and from others. It brings the chin up a quarter inch, for one. But it's also an act of self-love. It helps you remember who you are and what you represent.

What are your positive attributes? What's still on the shelf? Write them down. When you know what those attributes are, their truth bolstered by input from others, the Bar Car isn't as necessary. You can counter those "stories" about your many character flaws. You'll find that there's far less to escape and so much more to tap into. You can spend time elsewhere.

It's hard to find your way out of your head and out of the Bar Car, but finding people who get it can help. My attempt to leave brought me to Bob Palmer. Before he passed, he lived up in Pacific Palisades, and every Saturday I'd pick him up. We'd go to a meeting and then out to brunch. Instead of *Tuesdays with Morrie*, it was Saturdays with Bob. We'd sit for hours, drinking coffee, shooting the shit. We both loved horses and cowboys, and we'd tell each other stories of riding and visiting ranches as young men.

And all the while, he was teaching me to be more patient with myself. Kinder, more loving. He was showing me how to be on my own side. To always find something to laugh about. He was a key part of the tribe I built to help me see my worth, and he did the same for many others. I miss him every day.

Bob had a certain sparkle in his eye, a fire in his belly, and a peace of mind you could feel. He truly wanted to help people. He was out for the good of everyone. Those are the people you want to look for: the helpers. My mom is a helper. When I reached my twenty-fifth anniversary of sobriety, my mom and Cass came down to L.A. to help me celebrate, and they got to meet Bob. My mom instantly adored Bob and they all hit it off swimmingly. There was a mutual love and respect.

Today I try to share Bob's teachings, and his impact, not just with my mentees, but with everyone I work with. Bob didn't believe in weaknesses. Bob would say, "James, we all have strengths and we all have vulnerabilities." I like that. There's a softness in that saying that represents all Bob's love, wisdom, and gentleness. It's not often that we get that kind of messaging in life.

That's why I like to think of myself as less of a life coach and more of a life cheerleader. You already have the playbook. It's inside you. I am just here to help you crack it open.

One of the greatest management techniques I've ever learned came from my late dog trainer, Jonathan Klein. When I'm working with my mentees or my team, I'm all about positive reinforcement. Jonathan didn't believe in punishment.

He explained that if you come home to find that your dog has torn your shoe apart, trying to correct the behavior by swatting him on the nose isn't going to benefit him at all. He doesn't know why you're doing it; he chewed that shoe hours ago. All he knows is that you're hitting him. Instead, you keep your shoes where he can't get to them and give him bones and appropriate things to chew and encourage that. People are the same way—if you berate them for their bad behavior, all they can focus on is the fact that you're whacking them. But when you focus on the good they are doing, what's good about them, when you offer encouragement and coaching, the outcome is entirely different. People and dogs alike want to be part of the pack, part of the tribe. They want to have a role, to be heard, to be recognized, to feel important. And when they do, they can accomplish amazing things. They can let the other stuff fall away, listen to the whispers, and find a way forward. This works in all relationships.

I used to think I had to be tough to be a successful executive producer. I had to yell at people. Be the guy they feared. But I learned years ago that dealing in fear just makes you the lonely ogre in the corner office. When I switched to positivity—cheerleading over chastising—everything changed. When I began recognizing everyone, from my right hand to the receptionist, for their efforts, they began to consistently move the ball across the goal line, making things happen. The excuses and obstacles the Bar Car is stocked with just fell away. I could help others find their own way out because my tribe had helped me find mine.

Remember that there's value in the experiences you've had; they got you to where you are today. Then focus on the good stuff—the things that are working—to bring more of that into your life. That's how you trigger the Law of Attraction. You have to ask for what you want, believe that you'll get it, and make sure you're ready to receive it by cultivating positive emotions like love, joy, and gratitude. It's a shift in perception. And to make that shift, you may yet again have to reevaluate and adjust those stories you've been telling. To seek out people who can help you do that.

You have to go where you get fed, and the Bar Car doesn't serve dinner. But when you find the people who really nourish you—and when you can do that for others—you can get back to fine-tuning your engine, shoveling coal, and moving toward something bigger and better than you had previously imagined.

CHAPTER 8

The Caboose

FROM THE DECK OF THE Caboose, you can see the full length of the train ahead of you, chugging along toward the horizon. Looking up, you see the continuous puffs of smoke trailing the engine, the only visible sign of the effort it takes to power that colossal machine. Those great clouds of steam quickly dissipate into the flawless blue of the sky. You hold on to the railing to steady yourself, and stare through the connecting doors of every car in front of you.

Through the next set of doors is the Bar Car and all its distractions: music and laughter and gin-muddled conversation, muted by the distance and the sound of wheels turning over tracks.

You know the Dining Car is next in line, offering you the chance to refuel, to take care of yourself. If you breathe deeply, you can smell its offerings, lingering just beneath the vanilla scent of the ponderosa pines that flow past.

You close your eyes and imagine the peace of the Observation Car, how quiet it is compared to the all-encompassing roar that's engulfing you now. And you picture the Baggage Car, housing everything you've picked up along the way. You think about how it might feel to pull into the next station and heave some of those bags—slights, mistakes, abuse, and more—onto the platform and just pull away, watching them fade into the distance.

With your eyes still closed, you can see the Passenger Car too. It's full of the people and relationships that have shaped you, for better and for worse, your memories of them tethered to a whole gamut of emotions—pain and abuse, love and encouragement. They've all combined to make you who you are.

As you grip the railing, you can almost feel the heat from the furnace near the Coal Car, singeing the hair on your arms as you dump load after load into the roaring fire, the strain causing your biceps to bulge. You feel a sense of satisfaction in the knowledge that you're the one powering this tremendous beast, moving it forward one shovelful at a time.

Lastly, there's the engine—right in front, driving it all, the purpose behind the power.

But back here, you can appreciate the distance the Caboose provides. You don't have to focus on the action of every car, or weighing individual pieces of baggage, choosing from an overwhelming menu of dinner options, or navigating your relationships. Instead, you can just breathe. And you're overcome by how seamlessly everything works together, a single unit trudging onward, pulled by sheer grit and the miracle of momentum.

Taking the time to walk all the way to the back of the train can help you stay on track—headed in the direction of the sunset. In fact, from back here, you can see it all a bit more clearly. The mountains you're approaching look farther away. You can see their valleys and their peaks, the way the vegetation changes with the elevation. The sun drops a little lower and the sky begins to pinken, the bottoms of the distant clouds turning a brilliant, silvery blue. From here, you can take it all in. But it's not always easy to head to the Caboose, to let go of every little thing happening on board.

One of my guys called me the other day. Overall, things were really working out for him. He had a meaningful career, a beautiful family, and a comfortable home. But all he could focus on were the things in his life that *weren't* on track—this minor issue at work, that problem at his kid's school, an argument he and his wife had had over dinner the night before. He was frustrated. And with every issue he named, another one popped into his head—a stream of minor annoyances he felt were threatening to wreck everything he had built.

"You know," I told him, "it's like you're staring at a deer turd on the trail. All you have to do is look up and see the magnificent Yosemite Valley, Half Dome glistening in the morning sun, the towering granite cliffs of El Capitan providing shade to half of the valley. Yosemite Falls gushing from the High Sierra, the Merced River winding through the meadow and the pines." (If you haven't been to Yosemite National Park, go! It is one of the most beautiful places on God's green earth.)

It took me a long time to stop getting so hung up on the stuff that wasn't working. Instead, I let it derail me time after time. But after some years and distance, finding a better view from the Caboose, focusing on what was working became a whole lot easier.

Back when I was making my first movie, I approached my dad for help. It wasn't the first time I had asked him for help. I had come to him once before, right after I dropped out of college. I knew how well he had done for himself, and I knew that a few thousand dollars wouldn't make a difference to him. I just needed a little assistance to get back on my feet, I told him.

"Nah," he had said, "you have to do it yourself, like I did."

I thought this time might be different, though. I had a clear vision—one I thought was pretty good—and a plan for how to execute it. I worked up the guts to ask him, and when he saw how excited I was about the project, he asked me how much I needed.

"$5,000 should cover everything," I said.

"Tell you what," he said, "I'll write you a check. But this is a loan, not a gift. You need to pay me back. In full. ASAP."

I agreed to his terms, and we set up a payment schedule to ensure that he'd get his money back. But after my brief brush with success and the excitement of the film festivals died down, the reality of my situation set in. I didn't have a job. I was broke. There was no way I could make that first payment.

I called my dad to deliver the news, rattling off all the reasons for my financial limitations.

"I'm sorry," I said. "I just don't have it right now."

He was furious.

"You're a con artist," he told me. The next thing I heard was the clatter of the phone slamming into the receiver.

It was the only money he had ever lent me, and he'd called me a con artist. I felt my own rage rise. My dad had abandoned me time and again, and this was just another example. He didn't want to hear about my life or my problems. He didn't want to help. He didn't want to have anything to do with me. All the fight in me that I'd cultivated from clashes with my brothers and stepbrothers, with my stepdad, with the kids in the neighborhood—all of it bubbled up. I wasn't about to let my dad have the last word. I called him back and let loose a despicable barrage of invective, telling him exactly who I thought he was before hanging up on him.

I was breathing hard, shaking, seething, when my phone rang again. This time it was my stepmom, and she delivered her own horrible laundry list of claims against my character. I was banned from their house forever, she told me.

"Keep that $5,000. Consider it your inheritance."

It would be the last time any of us talked for ten years.

To be honest, I was ashamed of my behavior. I tried to seek forgiveness. I wrote letters of apology, trying to make it right. But my words, my rage had been so hurtful, I was afraid the damage was irreparable.

Five or six years later, when I got married, I extended an invitation to them, asking them to come to my engagement party. They said that they were going to be out of the country, but I found out they were in town. They didn't come to the wedding either. And over time, the bad blood—slights big and small—just built and built.

When my dad developed lung cancer, I didn't know what to do, how to overcome all the thorns in our relationship and get the conversation going again. For a while, I did nothing.

But then my brother Bobby called to tell me how bad it had gotten.

"You know Dad's dying," he said.

I swallowed hard. I didn't want that conversation from ten years earlier to be the last one we'd ever have.

"How long does he have?" I asked.

"They don't think it'll be more than a couple of days," he said.

"Maybe I can go see him in the hospital," I said. I knew my stepmother didn't want me in their house. I figured we could say our goodbyes in a hospital room at a time when she wasn't around—just me and Dad on neutral, sterile ground.

"He's at home, James," my brother said. "Hospice is there."

I asked him, "Do you think you could ask Trudi if I could come by if I fly up to Sacramento?"

"Of course."

Thankfully, Trudi agreed, and I booked a last-minute ticket. My brother David met me at the airport. It was pissing down rain as we drove up to my dad's house, the wipers sloshing torrents from the windshield. Wind slapped against the trees, threatening to send them into the road. When we got there, we ran from the car to the house, getting half-soaked in the process.

Trudi answered the door with a weak smile and offered me a hug.

"He doesn't know you're here," she whispered, her half smile turning to a conspiratorial grin.

The three of us walked down the hall toward his room, and I gingerly poked my head around the corner. Dad's eyes got wide when he saw me. I knew he thought I was still the kid I had been ten years earlier, attacking him over the phone. But so much had changed. So much water under that bridge. And there was so little time left. I walked in and took a seat in the lone chair next to his bed. Trudi motioned for everyone to leave the room.

"Hey, Dad," I said, placing my palm on his bed.

He looked at the rain, then at me, shaking his head. Once we knew it was just us, and that we were cool, he reached out. There was a pulse oximeter clamped around one finger, but he curled the rest of them around my hand. Outside, the rain pounded against the window, blurring everything beyond it.

"Ah shit, Jimmy," he said, knowing the end was near and that we'd lost so much time. It hadn't been an easy relationship, but we'd shared so much. He was still my dad.

My dad had been a member of the Sonoma County Trail Blazers for thirty-five years, and had even served as a past president. The Trail Blazers was a group united by a love for ranching and horses, and that's how members spent much of their time together. Every year in June, 350 men would head out to a big, beautiful ranch in the middle of nowhere. They'd set up camp in a meadow and erect a huge tent that housed the commissary. Next to that, they set up a proper stage. And next to that was the most important part: the bar. They'd go on daily trail rides and have cookouts, put on plays, dance, and drink, and the younger cowboys would fight and wrestle in the dust and mud. The rule was when you got thrown over the bar, you had to go to bed. It was just like the Wild West. There were men from all walks of life: judges, lawyers, carpenters, teachers, and plumbers.

I was the only one of my dad's kids who had really cowboyed; I had worked on a few cattle ranches around Northern California and Salinas, and had done some competitive team penning and team roping in and around Sacramento for a few years. Dad invited me to come as his guest on the trail ride. It was an absolute honor. It was a prestigious affair. On the ride, he had gotten a chance to see me rodeo and work cattle—stuff he loved to do too. And we had been able to move beyond the superficial, to bond as father and son. Thinking back on those times made me sad that we had spent so many years not talking.

David and I stayed in Auburn for four days, just sitting by Dad's side, talking to him as he drifted in and out of consciousness. I realized the ugly parts of our history weren't as important as I had once thought—the feelings of abandonment, the fighting, the frustration. He'd be gone soon, and we couldn't change the past. But we had that chance to make living amends, to remember that we had been important to each other, that there was love there.

Eventually, I had to go back to work. I held his hands in mine and kissed his forehead as he slept. Then I headed for the airport, grateful. I had so many friends who hadn't had the chance to do what I'd gotten to do. They'd found themselves looking for closure over headstones or on mountaintops, searching for a way to connect with someone who wasn't there anymore.

Dad died not long after I landed back in L.A.

I am eternally grateful to Trudi for having afforded me that important time with my father in his final days. I am not sure I would be the man I am today without it.

*   *   *

Loss can't help but show you what really matters.

A handful of years later, Bob Palmer, who had shown me what a father could really be, would be gone too. Bob's son Chris had died, and his wife—the love of his life—had passed just three months later; his heart had had enough. He only lived another couple of years after that. We got to spend a lot of quality time during those final years, but his heart eventually started to give out. Bob ended up in the hospital for months. All the guys he'd mentored, including Clay Tatum, Mike Binder, and myself, would rotate shifts, making sure someone came to see him every day. Finally, he told us he was ready to go home.

"I'm done with this," he said. "I want to be with my dogs. I want to sit in my backyard."

Hospitals are not in the business of discharging sick people, and the staff of this one certainly wasn't interested in letting Bob go.

"He can't just leave," his doctor argued. "He needs to stay in the bed. The machines, the medicines—they're keeping him alive."

But Bob had expressed his wishes, and it was up to us to make them happen.

"He's going home. Tell us what we need to do to get him there," Clay said. "Otherwise, I'm just going to back my fucking truck up and wheel his bed into the back."

Bob's doctor finally relented. We were going to be able to give him what he wanted. We finagled an ambulance to transport us back to his house. We were also going to need a nurse to help get him home.

I headed to the nurses' station down the hall from his room and asked, "Are any of you off in the next six hours? Want to make a quick thousand bucks?"

There were smiles all around as they rolled Bob's bed out of the hospital room and into the ambulance. Hospice would be there to meet him when he arrived. In the end, he got to be with his dogs, comfortable and content and sitting in the sunshine of his backyard. It was a beautiful sight. He died three days later.

The night he passed I was sitting in his living room with his daughter, Tracy, and his grandchildren Cody and Dylan.

"James," Tracy said, "Do you think you can get some of Bob's guys to come over to the house?"

"You sure you want to do that? It's kind of soon," I said.

"Yeah. I think he'd want that."

I nodded. I sent a text to the guys, letting them know what had happened and that we were going to do something to honor his life. The responses came flooding in:

"I'll be there."

"Count me in."

"I'm on my way."

We moved all the furniture from the house out into the backyard, making a huge circle around the lawn. The guys began to arrive. Car after car pulled up, parking in the driveway and along the street, eventually wrapping around the block. Some of the guys brought newcomers, people who had never met Bob but knew how special he was. Seventy-two people showed up that night. They were sitting on lawn chairs and stools and couches, even on the edge of the fence.

Tracy went to Bob's room to get his candle, the one he used to meditate. As everyone settled in to their seats in the dark, she lit it. I set the candle down on the table in front of the family, watching the flame flicker and wave, and every single person in that backyard—even the guys who didn't know him—shared something about Bob. The ones who hadn't met him talked about his impact, how his message had reached them in one way or another, though they'd never been introduced. The other men shared how they were better men for knowing Bob. How their children benefited from Bob's example. He had taught us so much. He'd touched so many lives.

Here was the inventory—the stuff that remained on the shelves even after he was gone. When the last person had finished, the candle went out on its own, a little wisp of smoke curling up from the wick. In that moment, I knew—we all knew—that Bob was still there. His friendship, his memory were here for good, for me and for so many others.

Bob's family asked me to speak at the funeral. The eulogists were Bob's dear friends Sir Anthony Hopkins, Dick Van Dyke, and me. I strained through the tears and managed to get this out:

Thank you, Tracy, for sharing your father with me. Cody, Dylan, and Sofia, thank you for sharing your Papa with me.

I was extremely lucky to have known Bob for the past twenty years. He was my sponsor, mentor, and most important, my friend. I loved Bob beyond words. He was closer to me than my own father. If I could have designed my own father and mashed him up with the Buddha, that was Bob. He was so full of love, wisdom, compassion, understanding, and patience. He was genuine, authentic, sincere, and he had the best damn sense of humor. He was a great teacher. He said things to me that I still hear in my head in his gentle, loving voice.

When I would get riled up about something, he would look at me, smile, and say, "It's just not that important."

When I would be hard on myself, it was, "Be on your own side, kid."

He meditated every day and would gladly share his technique of sitting down, lighting a candle, and repeating his mantra, "I am here, as I am. So am I."

After talking about heavy stuff, he always brought levity to the conversation, reminding me that everything was going to be OK. Always. He would often tell you a funny anecdote involving some interaction he had, and it usually involved someone who has a star on Hollywood Boulevard. Years ago Bob had written something that he had asked his friend Harvey Korman to read. Later, when Bob asked Harvey what he had thought, Harvey replied, "Bob . . . you talk better than you write."

Bob touched the lives of countless men and women. He has impacted careers and influenced some of the finest show-business talent we have ever known. He helped hundreds, if not thousands, of broken men get their lives back on track. He has helped us be better sons, fathers, husbands, brothers, employees, and always with a gentle word and a hug. We belong to an elite group where "Love and Service" is our code. Bob embodied that. The day after his beloved wife, Nancy, passed, he showed up at a meeting with a newcomer. Bob had what I want.

Bob was one of the only people in my life who really knew me and saw who I was. I am truly a much better man for knowing him and for spending every Saturday afternoon with him at Mayberry. I would call Bob every day on my way into the office; it has been an emotional commute these past few weeks. I will miss that the most.

We both loved horses and cowboys, and would often tell stories of visiting ranches and riding horses as young men. When I turned twenty-five years sober this year, he wrote this to me:

"If I was a lonely old cowboy lookin' for a tolerable trail partner gifted with brains, guts, warmth, and humor, I'd look your way and stop, James. Twenty-five years? Good start. I love you, Bob"

Harvey Korman was wrong. Bob wrote as well as he spoke.

While Bob was in the hospital I asked him if he wanted to leave a message, and he said yes. Here is what he said:

"All of you who can hear me, I can see your faces. I love you all so much. We hear that a lot, and we wonder how deep it goes. It can't go any deeper. It can't go any deeper, period. I feel your love, and when I'm gone, I will feel your love."

Well, now you get to ride off into the sunset, cowboy, and it was a great movie. You will always live in my heart. I am honored to have called you my friend. I will miss you greatly.

* * *

As you stand there, on the edge of your Caboose, looking over the whole of your train, take a second. Wherever you are in life, you've worked hard to power yourself this far. You are a survivor, shoveling coal day in and day out. You continue to do the work, both when life's blissful and when it's hard. That's powerful.

There's something I've learned on my own journey: whenever we compare ourselves to others, we lose—every time. When I compare myself to others—whether to build myself up or break myself down—I lose every time.

This train is your own. This is *your* journey, *your* path, *your* life. It's up to you to figure out how to make that long, arduous trek from your head to your heart—to find out what you're here to do, and lay the tracks to get you there. When Tom Brady is throwing darts to Julian Edelman, he's not questioning his career choice. He's right where the universe intends for him to be, doing what God built him to do. The same goes for people like Oprah Winfrey, Bill and Melinda Gates and my old friend Bob. But it's not just celebrities, or those whose mark on the world you can see. Everyone has that in them: God, fate, destiny—a higher purpose. When you find it, everything starts to make sense.

This country was founded on the pursuit of happiness: the idea that your path is valid and extraordinary and important, simply because it's yours.

Recognize your greatness. Embrace your own journey. And know that I'm here, ready to walk beside you. Just like the last stake at Promontory Point, Utah, that united the East and West—for good, our tracks eventually cross paths. That energy brings us together, to the people and communities that help drive us forward.

Whether or not we ever physically meet, we're connected. There is energy flowing between you and me—permeating all the cells and space between us. Always has been; always will be. I'll be here through the fear and doubts that prevent you from becoming the amazing you that God and the universe intended. And I'm cheering you on, every step of the way.

This is the time to step back and reflect. To appreciate how far you've come. Remember, taking stock of yourself is more than noting what you've sold or lost; it's about remembering what's left on the shelves. I'm willing to bet there's a lot more in you than you think.

Every day provides a new opportunity to learn more about your engine, to unload baggage, to spend more time shoveling coal than standing in the Bar Car. But just like those great steam locomotives, no matter how much work you have to do to get where you want to go, you're already greater than the sum of your parts. Your train is complete. It is whole and you are loved. Keep that in mind.

And as Bob always said, find something to laugh about.

Now, go be amazing!

My Old "Stories"

_____

_____

_____

_____

_____

_____

_____

_____

The New Story I Want to Tell Is...

_____

_____

_____

_____

_____

_____

_____

_____

Acknowledgments

THANK YOU TO BOB PALMER, who inspired me to start writing sooner rather than later, and who taught me much of the "good stuff" this book offers. Thank you to my incredible fiancée, Elisabeth, who fully supported me and encouraged me to tell my story so that I might help others as unselfishly as she does.

I'd also like to thank Clay Tatum and Jamie Benincasa for continuing to serve as excellent examples of the principles in this book. A shout-out to the Westside men's crew for their love and support.

I want to list the important teachers, mentors, and authors who have contributed to my message and voice: don Miguel Ruiz, William James, Dr. Carl Jung, Dr. William Silkworth, Bill Wilson, Dr. Bob Smith, Eric Balme, Jimmy Conway, Fr. Tom Weston, Robert Blye, James Hillman, Michael Meade,

Dr. Steve Ott, Jerry Aull, Sam and Sharon Anapolsky, Bruce Anapolsky, Bruce and Gayla Mace, Noradele Veronis, Ross and Simone Perich, Jamie and Tiffany Benincasa, Jack Osbourne, and Joe Manganiello.

Thank you to the men and women who continue to inspire me to stay healthy and pursue this work: Sharon Osbourne, another badass mom who overcame adversity to succeed; Dwayne "The Rock" Johnson, my fitness and business guy; Oprah Winfrey, my show business and humanity guru; Bill and Melinda Gates, my philanthropy models; Richard Branson, my business and management guru; Sugar Ray Leonard, who inspired me to tell the whole truth, as painful as it was, and who taught me I am a champion too.

And a final thank you to Michael Levin for helping me to organize my thoughts and words into a solid work.

To learn more about my talks, workshops, and seminars, please visit:

www.jamessweigert.com.

*Shoot me an email and tell me
the new story you want to tell!*

Made in the
USA
Columbia, SC